# THE INDIAN MUSALMANS

# THE INDIAN MUSALMANS.

BY

W. W. HUNTER, LL.D.

GYAN

*Published by*

GYAN

Gyan Publishing House
5, Ansari Road
Daryaganj, New Delhi-110002
Phone: 011-47034999, 9811692060
E-mail: books@gyanbooks.com

*Distribution Network*
gyanbooks.com
India, USA, Canada, UK, Australia, France



ISBN: 978-81-212-7320-6 (PB)
First Published, 1871

2nd Impression 2023

*Printed at:* Gyan Press, Delhi.



**THE INDIAN MUSALMANS**
Author: W. W. HUNTER

# THE INDIAN MUSALMANS.

BY

W. W. HUNTER, LL.D.

DIRECTOR-GENERAL OF STATISTICS TO THE GOVERNMENT OF INDIA,

ONE OF THE COUNCIL OF THE ASIATIC SOCIETY OF BENGAL, HONORARY FELLOW OF THE ETHNOL. SOC. LONDON, AND OF THE ROYAL INSTITUTE OF NETHERLANDS INDIA AT THE HAGUE, ETC.

*SECOND EDITION.*

LONDON:

TRÜBNER AND COMPANY.

1872.

# DEDICATION.

SIMLA, 23*d June* 1871.

MY DEAR HODGSON,

I DEDICATE this little book to you in acknowledgment of the benefit which I have derived from your labours. You, of all the scholars whom our Service has produced, have most fully recognised the duty of studying the people. The greatest wrong that the English can do to their Asiatic subjects is not to understand them. The chronic peril which environs the British Power in India is the gap between the Rulers and the Ruled. In these pages I have tried to bring out in clear relief the past history and present requirements of a persistently belligerent class—of a class whom successive Governments have declared to be a source of permanent danger to the Indian Empire.

I am,

Yours sincerely,

W. W. HUNTER.

BRIAN HOUGHTON HODGSON, ESQ.,
Alderney Grange, Gloucestershire.

# PREFACE TO THE SECOND EDITION.

A GREAT public calamity has given most mournful emphasis to these pages. Five days before the first copies reached Calcutta, a Musalmán assassin struck down the Chief-Justice of Bengal under the portico of his own Court. I put forth this Second Edition in the hope that it may produce a reaction equally apart from the popular alarm which has followed that crime, and from the popular apathy which had for years preceded it. To know the real truth about our position in India, seems to me to be the sole safeguard against chronic torpor on the one hand, and sudden panics on the other.

A critic, whose article proves that he knows India well, and whose eloquent appreciation has given me much encouragement, speaks of the work as a 'demi-official' one. I cannot let the revised sheets go home without guarding against the misconception to which such a statement might give rise. Government granted me free access to its Archives on a subject in which it was known I had long taken a deep interest, and with regard to which it seemed well that the whole facts should be placed before the public. But it made no attempt to influence my views, nor is it in any way responsible for my conclusions. All that this book does is to collect the documents hitherto isolated in the various Departments of the Government of India, and out of these scattered links to put together a trustworthy historical narrative.

SIMLA, 3d *October* 1871.

# CONTENTS.

## CHAPTER I.



## CHAPTER II.



## CHAPTER III.



## CHAPTER IV.



## APPENDIX.

# THE INDIAN MUSALMANS.

## CHAPTER I.

### THE STANDING REBEL CAMP ON OUR FRONTIER.

THE Bengal Muhammadans are again in a strange state. For years a Rebel Colony has threatened our Frontier; from time to time sending forth fanatic swarms, who have attacked our camps, burned our villages, murdered our subjects, and involved our troops in three costly Wars. Month by month, this hostile Settlement across the border has been systematically recruited from the heart of Bengal. Successive State Trials prove that a network of conspiracy has spread itself over our Provinces, and that the bleak mountains which rise beyond the Panjáb are united by a chain of treason-depots with the tropical swamps through which the Ganges merges into the sea. They disclose an organization which systematically levies money and men in the Delta, and forwards them by regular stages along our high-roads to the Rebel Camp two thousand miles off. Men of keen intelligence and ample fortune have embarked in the plot, and a skilful system of remittances has reduced one of the most perilous enterprises of treason to a safe operation of banking.

While the more fanatical of the Musalmáns have thus engaged in overt sedition, the whole Muhammadan community has been openly deliberating on their obligation to rebel. During the past nine months, the leading newspapers in Bengal have filled their columns with discussions as to the duty of the Muhammadans to wage war against the Queen. The collective wisdom of the Musalmán Law Doctors of Northern India was first promulgated in a formal Decision (Fatwa). Next the Bengal Muhammadans put forth a pamphlet on the question; and even the Shiah sect, a comparatively small body in India, have not been able to restrain themselves from print. For some months the Anglo-Indian Press was inclined to smile at the pains which the loyal sort of Musalmáns were taking to ascertain whether they could abstain from rebellion without perdition to their souls. But the universal promulgation of formal Legal Decisions by the Muhammadan Law Doctors, soon convinced our countrymen that the subject might have a serious as well as a ludicrous aspect. The cumulative papers now published—papers drawn up and issued by the Muhammadans themselves—leave not a shadow of doubt as to the danger through which the Indian Empire is passing. They will convince every reasonable mind, that while the more reckless among the Musalmáns have for years been engaged in overt treason, the whole community has been agitated by the greatest State Question that ever occupied the thoughts of a people. The duty of rebellion has been formally and publicly reduced to a nice point of Muhammadan Law. Somehow or other, every Musalmán seems to have found himself called on to declare his faith; to state, in the face of his co-religionists, whether he will or will not contribute to the

Traitors' Camp on our Frontier; and to elect, once and for all, whether he shall play the part of a devoted follower of Islám, or of a peaceable subject of the Queen. In order to enable the Muhammadans to decide these points, they have consulted not only the leading Doctors of their Law in India, but they have gone as far as Mecca itself. The obligation of the Indian Musalmáns to rebel or not rebel, hung for some months on the deliberations of three priests in the Holy City of Arabia.

I propose to exhibit this spirit of unrest among our Musalmán subjects in the threefold form which it has assumed. I shall briefly narrate the events which led to the settlement of a Rebel Colony on our Frontier, and lay before the reader a few of the chronic disasters in which it has involved the British Power. In my second chapter I shall explain the treasonable organization by which the Rebel Camp has drawn unfailing supplies of money and men from the interior Districts of the Empire. I shall then unfold the legal discussions to which this anomalous state of things has given rise,—discussions which disclose the Muhammadan masses eagerly drinking in the poisoned teachings of the Apostles of Insurrection, while a small minority anxiously seeks to get rid of the duty to rebel by ingenious interpretations of the Sacred Law. But if I were to end here, I should have only told half the truth. The Musalmáns of India are, and have been for many years, a source of chronic danger to the British Power in India. For some reason or other they hold aloof from our system, and the changes in which the more flexible Hindus have cheerfully acquiesced, are regarded by them as deep personal wrongs I propose, therefore, in my fourth chapter, to inquire into the grievances of the Muhammadans under English Rule; to point out their real wrongs, and the means of remedying them.

The Rebel Camp on the Panjáb Frontier owes its origin to Sayyid Ahmad,[1] one of those bold spirits whom our extermination of the Pindárí Power scattered over India half a century ago. He began life as a horse soldier in the service of a celebrated freebooter,[2] and for many a year harried the rich opium-growing villages of Málwá. The stern order which the rising power of the Sikhs under Ranjit Singh imposed on their Musalmán neighbours, made the trade of a Muhammadan bandit a perilous and an unprofitable one. At the same time, their strict Hinduism fanned the zeal of the Muhammadans of Northern India into a flame. Sayyid Ahmad wisely suited himself to the times, gave up robbery, and about 1816 went to study the Sacred Law under a Doctor of high repute at Dehli.[3] After a three years' noviciate he started forth as a preacher, and by boldly attacking the abuses which have crept into the Muhammadan faith in India, obtained a zealous and turbulent following. The first scene of his labours lay among the descendants of the Rohillás,[4] for whose extermination we had venally lent our troops fifty years before, and whose sad history forms one of the ineffaceable blots on Warren Hastings' career. Their posterity have, during the past half century, taken an undying revenge, and still recruit the Rebel Colony on our Frontier with its bravest swordsmen. In the case of the Rohillás, as in many other instances where we have done wrong in India, we have reaped what we sowed.

[1] A native of the British District of Rái Barelí. Born in the sacred month Muharram of 1201 A.H., or 1786 A.D.

[2] Amír Khán Pindárí, afterwards Nuwáb of Tank.

[3] Sháh Abd-ul-azíz, of whom more hereafter.

[4] In the Jágir of Faiz-ullah Khán, towards Rámpur in Rohilkhand.

During 1820 the Apostle journeyed slowly southwards, his disciples rendering him menial services in acknowledgment of his spiritual dignity, and men of rank and learning running like common servants, with their shoes off, by the side of his palanquin. A protracted halt at Patna so swelled the number of his followers as to require a regular system of Government. He appointed agents to go forth and collect a tax from the profits of trade in all the large towns which had lain on his route. He further nominated four Khalífs,[1] or Spiritual Vicegerents, and a high priest, by a formal Deed such as the Muhammadan Emperors used in appointing governors of provinces. Having thus formed a permanent centre at Patna, he proceeded towards Calcutta, following the course of the Ganges, making converts and appointing agents in every important town by the way. In Calcutta the masses flocked to him in such numbers, that he was unable even to go through the ceremony of initiation by the separate laying on of hands. Unrolling his turban, therefore, he declared that all who could touch any part of its ample length became his disciples. In 1822 he made a religious journey to Mecca; and having thus completely covered his former character as a robber beneath the sacred garb of a pilgrim, he returned in October of the following year, by Bombay. Here his success as a preacher was as great as it had been in Calcutta. But a more congenial field lay before the freebooter-saint than the peaceful population of an English Presidency town. On his way back to Northern India, he enlisted a vast

[1] Maulaví Wiláyat Alí; Maulaví Ináyat Alí; Maulaví Murhum (Marhamat?) Alí; and Maulaví Furhat Husain; besides Sháh Muhammad Husain as chief priest.

turbulent following[1] in his native District of Barelí; and in 1824 made his appearance among the wild mountaineers of the Peshάwar Frontier, preaching a Holy War against the rich Sikh towns of the Panjáb.

The Pathán tribes responded with frantic enthusiasm to his appeal. These most turbulent and most superstitious of the Muhammadan peoples were only too delighted to get a chance of plundering their Hindu neighbours under the sanction of religion. The Sikhs, most aggressive of modern Hindu races, at that time ruled the Panjáb, and the Apostle assured the fanatic Musalmán borderers that those who survived would return laden with booty, while those who fell would be translated in a moment to Heaven as martyrs of the Faith. He travelled through Kandahar and Cabul, raising the country as he went, and consolidating his influence by a skilful coalition[2] of the tribes. Their avarice was enlisted by splendid promises of plunder; their religion, by the assurance that he was divinely commissioned to extirpate the whole Infidel world, from the Sikhs even unto *the Chinese*. To the grave political leaders of the mountains, the worldly-minded heads of tribes, he expatiated on the necessity of checking the rise of the adjoining Sikh Power, bitterly remembering his early debt of hatred against the Hindu Ranjit Singh. After thus arranging for the success of a religious manifesto, he issued, in the name of God, a formal summons to all devout Musalmáns to join the Holy War. 'The Sikh

[1] Who had been recruited by his high priest, Sháh Muhammad Husain.

[2] The Yusafzáís and Barakzáís were his staunchest followers. The Chief of Panjtar (Fathi Khán) afterwards joined him, and the important principality of Swát. He also established himself in the State of Amb. The Nuwáb of Tank, his former leader, always remained a source of supplies both in money and recruits.

nation,' runs this curious document, 'have long held sway in Lahor and other places. Their oppressions have exceeded all bounds. Thousands of Muhammadans have they unjustly killed, and on thousands they have heaped disgrace. No longer do they allow the Call to Prayer from the mosques, and the killing of cows they have entirely prohibited. When at last their insulting tyranny could no more be endured, Hazrat Sayyid Ahmad (may his fortunes and blessings ever abide!), having for his single object the protection of the Faith, took with him a few Musalmáns, and, going in the direction of Cabul and Pesháwar, succeeded in rousing Muhammadans from their slumber of indifference, and nerving their courage for action. Praise be to God, some thousands of believers became ready at his call to tread the path of God's service; and on the 21st December 1826,[1] the Jihád against the Infidel Sikhs begins.' Meanwhile the holy man's emissaries carried the Call to War throughout all the cities of Northern India where he had made disciples; and the above proclamation is taken from a tract published in the far inland Province of Oudh.[2]

A fanatical War, of varying success, against the Sikhs followed. Both sides massacred without mercy, and the bitter hatred between the Muhammadan Crescentaders and the Hindu Sikhs lives in a hundred local traditions. Ranjit Singh strengthened his Frontier by several of the skilful generals whom the breaking up of the Napoleonic armies had cast loose upon the world. The name of an Italian soldier of fortune, General Avitabili,[3] is still on

[1] The 20th Jumáda-'s-sániya, 1242 Hijra.

[2] The Targhíb-ul-Jihád, an incitement to religious war by a Maulaví of Kanauj. Official Proceedings, 1865.

[3] I give the spelling of his name and his nationality according to local tradition.

the lips of the Pesháwar peasantry. The Muhammadans burst down from time to time upon the plains, burning and murdering wherever they went. On the other hand, the bold Sikh villagers armed *en masse*, beat back the hill fanatics into their mountains, and hunted them down like beasts. The fierce passions of the time have left behind a land-tenure of a horrible nature—a Tenure by Blood. The Hindu borderers still display with pride a Grant for their village lands on payment of a hundred heads of the Husainkhail tribe as yearly rent.

In regular engagements the tumultuous Army of the Crescent proved no match for the disciplined cohorts of the Sikhs. In 1827 the Prophet led his bands against one of their entrenched Camps, and was repulsed with great slaughter. But the lowland general dared not follow up his victory. The fanatical bands fell back across the Indus into the mountains, and so increased their fame by guerilla successes, that the Sikh chief found himself compelled to buy the alliance of the very tribes who had been foremost in the raids. In 1829 the lowlanders trembled for the safety of Pesháwar itself, their Frontier Capital, and the Governor[1] basely attempted to put an end to the war by poisoning the Prophet. This rumour inflamed the zeal of the Muhammadan highlanders to a red heat. They burst down in fury on the plains, massacred the Infidel Army, and mortally wounded its general. Pesháwar was only saved by a force under Prince Sher Singh and General Ventura. The Prophet's influence had now spread as far as Kashmír, and troops from every discontented prince of Northern India flocked to his camp. Ranjit Singh, the head of the great Sikh confederacy, hurried up a force under his most skilful

[1] He was a Muhammadan, but the mere creature of the Sikh Ranjit Singh.

lieutenants. In spite of a reverse in June 1830,[1] the Apostolic Army occupied the plains in overwhelming force; and before the end of the year, Peshâwar itself, the Western Capital of the Panjáb, had fallen.

This marks the culminating point in the Prophet's career. He proclaimed himself Khalíf, and struck coins bearing the legend, 'Ahmad the Just, Defender of the Faith; the glitter of whose scimetar scatters destruction among the Infidels.' But the dismay caused by the fall of Pesháwar brought the matchless diplomacy of Ranjit Singh into the field. The wily Sikh detached the petty Muhammadan Principalities from the Army of the Crescent by separate appeals to their self-interest, and the Prophet found himself compelled to abandon the city on condition of a ransom being paid. The internal dissensions among his followers soon defied all control. His regular troops consisted of Hindustání fanatics, Muhammadans from the Indian Provinces, who accepted his fortunes for good or for evil, and who, in fact, would have found it impossible to desert him. The Army of the Crescent, however, was swollen with hosts of Frontier Patháns, who, with all the valour, possessed all the pride and avarice, of mountaineers. On one occasion, an important tribe of these borderers had deserted on the eve of battle,[2] and the fanatics had afterwards taken a severe retribution. The Prophet felt the necessity of liberality to the Hindustání followers, on whom he could always depend. At first he confined himself to levying tithes for their support from his Frontier adherents. This they bore with little reluctance, as a religious contribution to the good cause. But after both sides had been inflamed by such exac-

[1] By the Sikh Army under General Allard and Hari Singh Nalwá.
[2] The Barakzáís, at the engagement with the Sikhs near Saidi.

tions, the Prophet began to lose ground. His talents were rather those of a fanatical incendiary than of an impartial ruler of a great coalition, and the wonderful influence which he had acquired over the Frontier tribes soon showed signs of melting away. As he found his power waning, he had more frequently recourse to severities, and at length wounded the feelings of the mountaineers in their most tender point. He entered upon an ill-advised effort to reform the marriage customs of the highlanders, who practically sold their daughters in wedlock to the highest bidder; and as his Indian followers had left house and home, and were without wives, he issued an edict that every girl not married within twelve days should become the property of his lieutenants. The tribes rose and massacred his Hindustání retinue, and the Prophet himself narrowly escaped.[1] But his reign was over; and in 1831, while aiding one of his former lieutenants who had set up for himself, the Prophet was surprised by a Sikh Army under Prince Sher Singh, and slain.[2]

The religious character of the movement belongs to a later portion of this Work. Neither in India nor anywhere else can a religious leader stir the hearts of a people without a genuine belief in the goodness of his cause. In my next chapter I shall unfold the nobler aspects of Sayyid Ahmad's career. Meanwhile I have dwelt at

1 From Panjtar to the Valley of Paklí.

2 At Bálákot, in May 1831. I have collected the foregoing Account of Sayyid Ahmad from the Records of the Foreign Office and Home Department, Government of India, along with the evidence that has come out in the successive State Trials from 1852 to 1870, and from a valuable memorandum by Mr. T. E. Ravenshaw, late Magistrate of Patna. Several of the details will be found in Captain Cunningham's Work on the Sikhs. A writer, who has apparently used some of the same materials, has put forth a good account of the Wahábis in the *Calcutta Review*, vols. c., ci., and cii.

some length upon the origin of the Fanatical Settlement, because I propose very briefly to dismiss its further history, till it emerges in its present phase as a Rebel Camp on our own Frontier. Among the chief lieutenants of the Prophet were two brothers, grandsons of a notorious murderer[1] who had fled for his life to the mountains beyond the Indus, and there established himself as a hermit at Sittána. The refugee ascetic gradually acquired the veneration of the mountaineers, who made over to him the lands on which his hermitage stood, as an asylum and a neutral ground,—a very convenient provision among tribes constantly engaged in blood-feuds. One of his grandsons,[2] who had served as Treasurer to the Prophet, succeeded to the Village of Refuge at Sittána, and invited thither the remnants of the Apostolic Host.

About the same time, the religious head of the Principality of Swát, having taken alarm at the progress of the British Power, determined to strengthen himself by establishing a firm regal Government. He accordingly invited the other grandson[3] of the hermit to the Swát valleys, and made him King. By this means he fortified the natural valour of his subjects, by the assurance that, having now a hero of the Crescentade at the head of their troops, all who might fall in the apprehended conflict with the English or Hindu Infidels would enjoy a martyr's reward. The fears of the Swát tribes were not, however, destined to be realized; and their King reigned till 1857, when he died, and no successor was elected. His son,[4] now the head of the family, claims the leadership

[1] Zamín Sháh, a native of Takhtaband in Bonair.
[2] Sayyid Omar Sháh.
[3] Sayyid Akbar Sháh.
[4] Sayyid Mubárak Sháh.

of the Fanatical Host at Sittána, and asserts a wavering pretension to the realm of Swát.

In this way the fanatics firmly established a twofold power upon the Frontier, and by their emissaries among the superstitious border tribes, kept alive the embers of the Holy War. During intervals of many years they sank into the insignificance of border freebooters, but from time to time fired up into a fierce Army of the Crescent. They perpetrated endless depredations and massacres upon their Hindu neighbours before we annexed the Panjáb, annually recruiting their Camp with Muhammadan zealots from the British Districts. We took no precautions to prevent our subjects flocking to a Fanatical Colony which spent its fury on the Sikhs,—an uncertain coalition of tribes, sometimes our friends and sometimes our enemies. An English gentleman, who had large Indigo factories in our North-Western Provinces, tells me that it was customary for all pious Musalmáns in his employ to lay aside a fixed share of their wages for the Sittána Encampment. The more daring spirits went to serve for longer or shorter periods under the fanatic leaders. As his Hindu overseers every now and then begged for a holiday for the annual celebration of their father's obsequies, so the Muhammadan bailiffs were wont between 1830 and 1846 to allege the religious duty of joining the Crescentaders as a ground for a few months' leave.

For the remissness which thus permitted our subjects to join the Fanatic Host against our Sikh neighbours, we were destined to pay dear. The Prophet[1] had established

[1] By the 'Prophet' I invariably mean Sayyid Ahmad. Technically he was an *Imám* (Leader) from the political point of view, and a *Walí* (Favourite of God) from the theological one. Strictly speaking, the line of the true Prophets ended with Christ and Muhammad.

a regular system of Apostolic Successors, both in our territories and upon the Sikh Frontier. The movement was thus placed beyond the contingencies of the life or death of any of the individual leaders, and his own decease had been converted by the zeal of his followers into an apotheosis for the further spread of the Faith. Two of the Khalífs or Vicegerents whom he had appointed at Patna in 1821 made a pilgrimage to the Frontier, and ascertained that their leader's disappearance was a miracle; that indeed he was still alive, and would manifest himself in due time at the head of a Holy Army, and expel the English Infidels from India. His Deputies continued therefore to levy money and men, but especially money, in the chief towns along the valley of the Ganges where the Prophet had preached on his journey to Calcutta in 1820–22. A perennial stream of malcontents thus flowed from our territory to the Fanatic Colony. Absconding debtors, escaped convicts, spendthrifts too ruined to be at peace with social order, traitors too guilty to hope for mercy from the law,—all flocked from the British Plains to this cave of Adullam in the North. There were also refugees of a nobler sort, and every Muhammadan religionist too zealous to live quietly under a Christian Government, girded up his loins and made for the Sittána Camp. Their hand fell heaviest upon the Sikh villages, but they hailed with fierce delight any chance of inflicting a blow upon the English Infidel. They sent a great force to help our enemies in the Cabul War, and a thousand of them remained stedfast against us to the death In the fall of Ghazní alone, three hundred obtained the joys of martyrdom from the points of English bayonets.

On our annexation of the Panjáb, the fanatic fury,

which had formerly spent itself upon the Sikhs, was transferred to their successors. Hindus and English were alike Infidels in the eyes of the Sittána Host, and as such, were to be exterminated by the sword. The disorders which we had connived at, or at least viewed with indifference, upon the Sikh Frontier, now descended as a bitter inheritance to ourselves.

The records of the Patna Court show that the Vicegerents[1] early established a character for themselves on the Frontier as fanatical firebrands. In 1847, Sir Henry Lawrence recorded a proceeding[2] to the effect that they were well known as fighters for religion[3] in the Panjáb; and as such, they were forwarded under custody to their homes in Patna. The Magistrate there took security from them, and from two other of the most wealthy members of their sect, for their future good conduct. But in 1850 I find them preaching sedition in the Rájsháhí District of Lower Bengal, where they had also to give bonds to keep the peace, and on the repetition of their offence were twice turned out of the District.[4] In 1851, the same Vicegerents,[5] or successors of the Prophet, although bound, so far as parchment bonds and sureties could restrain them, to remain at their homes in Patna, were found disseminating treason on the Panjáb Frontier.[6]

In 1852 they deemed their plans ripe for execution. Money and men from our territory had poured into the Sittána Camp, and a treasonable correspondence with our

[1] Ináyat and Wiláyat Alí.

[2] Magistrates' Records, dated 13th April 1847.

[3] Ghozát or Mujáhidún. Their title of Wahábi belongs to a later period, and will be explained in Chapter II.

[4] Proceedings of the Magistrate of Rájsháhí, dated 23d February 1850.

[5] Ináyat and Wiláyat Alí.

[6] Proceeding of Board of Revenue, dated 12th May 1851.

troops was seized by the Panjáb authorities. Their leaders made a skilful attempt to tamper with the 4th Native Infantry, stationed at Ráwal Pindí, conveniently near to the Fanatic Colony; and one of the first Regiments which, on their invading our Province, would have been sent to act against them. The letters distinctly proved that they had established a regular organisation for passing up men and arms from Bengal to the Rebel Camp. At the same time the Patna Magistrate reported[1] that the rebel sect were upon the increase in that city. Sedition was openly preached by the principal inhabitants of this capital of a British Province. The police had leagued themselves with the fanatics; and one of their leaders[2] assembled seven hundred men in his house, and declared his resolve to resist any further investigation of the Magistrate by force of arms.

The British Government could no longer shut its eyes to the existence of a great treasonable organisation within its territories, for supplying money and men to the Fanatical Camp on the Frontier. During the autumn of 1852, Lord Dalhousie recorded two important Minutes on the subject. By the first he directed the internal organisation to be closely watched. The second had to deal with a proposition for a Frontier War against the border tribes, whose superstitious hatred to the Infidel the Hindustání fanatics had again fanned to a red heat. In the same year they attacked our ally, the Chief of the Amb State, and necessitated the despatch of a British force. In 1853, several of our native soldiers were convicted of correspondence with the traitors.

I do not propose to trace in detail the insults, raids, and murders which led to the Frontier War of 1858

[1] On the 19th of August 1852. [2] Maulaví Ahmad-ullah.

Throughout the whole period the fanatics kept the border tribes in a state of chronic hostility to the British Power. A single fact will speak volumes. Between 1850 and 1857 the Frontier disorders forced us to send out sixteen distinct expeditions, aggregating 33,000 Regular Troops; and between 1850 and 1863 the number rose to twenty separate expeditions, aggregating 60,000 Regular Troops, besides Irregular Auxiliaries and Police. During this time the Sittána Colony, although stirring up a perpetual spirit of fanaticism along the Frontier, had wisely avoided direct collision with our troops. They might secretly help the tribes whom they had incited against us, but they did not dare to wage war on their own account. But in 1857 they openly formed a coalition against us,[1] and had the audacity to call on the British authorities to help them in collecting their Black Mail. Incensed by our refusal, they came boldly down upon our territory, and made a night attack on the camp of Lieutenant Horne, the Assistant Commissioner, who scarcely escaped with his life. Retaliation could no longer be delayed, and General Sir Sidney Cotton entered the hills with an Army of 5000 men.[2] As this is only the first of several Wars into which the Fanatic Camp has plunged our Frontier, I propose to dismiss it briefly and to take the second—that of 1863—as an illustration of such campaigns. After some difficulties, our Column burned the villages of the rebel allies, razed or blew up the two most important forts, and destroyed the Traitor Settlement at Sittána. The fanatics, however, merely fell back into the fastnesses of the Mahában mountain; and so little had we shaken their power, that they immediately re-

[1] Particularly of the Yusafzái and Panjtar Tribes.

[2] Artillery, 219; Cavalry, 551; Infantry, 4107; total, 4877 Regular Troops.

ceived a new inner Settlement at Malká as a gift from a neighbouring tribe.[1]

The Fanatic Camp had other enemies, however, besides the British troops. Every now and then, in an access of religious self-confidence, they tried to levy tithes from the adjoining highland clans. According to the individual influence of the preacher who acted as the tax-gatherer, these exactions were submitted to, or evaded, or refused. A constant source of irritation thus smouldered among the mountains. We have seen how it alienated the tribes from the Prophet himself, and led to his desertion and death in 1831. When a clan refused tithes, the Fanatic Colony descended *en masse*, cut the crops of the recalcitrants, and carried off the harvest. In 1858 the tribal resistance against this religious taxation culminated in an attack upon Sittána itself, in which the fanatic leader[2] fell. The Rebel Settlement thus weakened, both by Sir Sidney Cotton's campaign and by the defection of its firmest allies, remained quiet for two years. We made over the Sittána lands to the tribe[3] which had resisted the tithing emissaries and slain the Fanatic chief. From this, and another adjoining clan,[4] we took engagements that they would never allow the fanatics to re-enter their territory, and that they would declare war on any third tribe which should endeavour to bring them in. They also bound themselves to prevent the fanatics or other desperate characters from passing through their country, on marauding expeditions against the British Frontier.

But scarcely two years elapsed before the Rebel

[1] The Amazáís.

[2] Sayyid Omar Sháh, killed by the Atmanzáí tribe.

[3] The Atmanzáís.

[4] The Jadúns.

Colony had regained its influence among the superstitious highland races. In 1861 they advanced from Malká, the interior retreat upon the Mahában, into which Sir Sidney Cotton had driven them in 1858, and fortified themselves[1] on a peak just above their old Settlement of Sittána. From this stronghold they burst down upon our villages; and the very tribes who had pledged themselves to prevent their ingress, gave them free passage through their territory on their kidnapping raids. As if to announce the return of the old state of things with a note of triumph, the fanatics descended upon our Ráwal Pindí District, and murdered two travellers in open day upon the high road, and almost within sight of a strong Police Station.[2] Three weeks later they again came down upon our territory, carried off three wealthy merchants, and coolly entered into a correspondence with our officers, demanding a ransom of Rs. 1550 for our captive subjects. Of this sum the fanatic leader was to receive one half. Another kidnapping inroad took place immediately after, in April 1861. The Frontier authorities reported that things had returned to the old disgraceful turbulence of 1858. It was in vain that the British officers appealed to the faith and to the fears of our allied tribes. Although several of their villages lay at our mercy, they cast in their lot with their co-religionists, and no course remained but retribution. We accordingly established a strict blockade of the offending tribes; completely cutting off their communication from the outside world, and taking prisoner any of them that ventured across the line. This brought them to reason. They again entered into engagements, and forced the Rebel Colony to retire from the Sittána territory to its interior fastness at Malká.

[1] At Sirí.

[2] On the 14th February 1861.

Nevertheless our disloyal Hindustání subjects continued to flock to the Traitors' Camp; and in 1862 their numbers had so increased that the Panjáb Government felt compelled to advise another Frontier War. Indeed, things had now reached such a height, that the Secretary of State declared his belief[1] that the rebels would have, sooner or later, to be expelled by force of arms, and that they were a lasting source of danger so long as they remained on our border. It was, however, impossible to undertake an expedition on the moment, and early in April 1863 we find them murdering and plundering within our territory. In July of that year they boldly re-occupied their Sittána Settlement, and sent threatening messages to our feudatory, the Chief of Amb. The neighbouring tribes again sacrificed their fidelity to their fanaticism, and scattered their engagements with us to the winds. The Traitor Colony was once more supreme upon the Frontier. On the 7th September 1863 the Fanatic Host came down upon British territory, and by a night attack upon the camp of our Guide Corps, gave the signal for open war. A week later they invaded our Amb Feudatory, destroyed his villages upon the Black Mountain, and gave battle to his outposts. In the same month they burst down on our friendly levies of Tanáwal, cutting up a native officer with a party of men. Not content with attacking our allies, they fired on our own pickets upon the banks of the Indus,[2] and in a formal manifesto declared war against the English Infidels, and summoned all good Musalmáns to the Crescentade.

We had therefore arrived at precisely the same state of affairs as that which in 1827–30 ended in the occupation of the Panjáb by the Fanatic Host, and the fall of

[1] Despatch of 7th April 1862.

[2] At Nawágirán.

the Frontier Capital. It became impossible any longer to avoid a War. Frontier campaigns, however, are little instructive as military performances, and they shed but small lustre upon the stronger Power. The ultimate issue of a conflict between a vast military Empire like British India, and a coalition of savage tribes, however brave and however strongly supported by religious zeal, cannot be doubtful. There is, moreover, a sameness about such operations, and a certainty in the severe retribution in which, sooner or later, they end, almost sickening to a Christian man. I shall therefore select only one of our expeditions against the Fanatic Colony for detailed description. It will be found, that as the Traitor Camp has been for years a cause of disgrace to our Frontier during peace, so it became a prolific source of disaster to our Armies in time of war. So long as we left it alone, it steadily sent forth bands to kidnap and murder our subjects and our allies: when we tried to extirpate it by arms, it baffled our leaders, inflicted severe losses on our troops, and for a time defied the whole Frontier Force of British India.

It is easy to understand how a Settlement of traitors and refugees, backed by the seditious and fanatical masses within our Empire, could, in an access of bigoted hatred, throw down the gauntlet. But it is difficult to comprehend how they could, even for a time, withstand the combined strategy and weight of a civilised Army. In order to explain this, it becomes necessary to briefly describe the country in which their Prophet had fixed the Headquarters of his militant sect.

In the extreme north of the Indus Valley, upon the boundary of the last tribe which owes allegiance to the British Crown, rises the Sacred Peak of the Hindus.

The Mahában, literally the Great Forest, that clothed its slopes, seems to have impressed the early Aryan immigrants more deeply than any other physical phenomenon which they met with on their primeval southern journey. It gave the name to the mountain itself; and the cluster of peaks and ranges, which tower to the height of 7400 feet on the west bank of the Indus, are still known as Mahában—the Great Forest. These peaks became to their race what Sinai was to the Jews. Sanskrit poetry crystallised the veneration of the primitive time, and for ages the Mahában has continued a place of pilgrimage among the devout Hindus. Amid those solemn heights Arjuna fought single-handed with the Great God,[1] and, although defeated like Jacob of old, won the Irresistible Weapon from the Deity. Happy was the ancient hermit who could lay his bones beneath the shadows of the Great Forest, where tradition affirmed that even the lesser divinities themselves were wont, by fasting and solitude, to cleanse such delicts as celestial natures may be capable of.[2]

In this retreat of primitive Hindu piety, a number of violent and superstitious Muhammadan tribes now dwell. Petty Principalities, not less fierce or less fanatical, occupy the Black Mountain on the other side of the Indus to the east, and demand the constant surveillance of an advanced British force at Abbottabad. The question of tithes, and similar spiritual exactions, prevent any permanent coalition with the Fanatical Settlement; but the tribes are liable to bursts of religious excitement, and are always delighted to get a chance of plundering the

[1] Mahádeva.

[2] Here, and in Chapter II., I have made use of an article which I put forth seven years ago in the *Calcutta Quarterly Review*.

rich Hindu villages within our Frontier. The Spiritual Principality, or, as it may be called, Muhammadan See of Swát, contains alone a population of 96,000, every man of whom is bred up in a hereditary apprehension of a British invasion, and in a conviction that if he must fight against the Infidels, it is wise to have a religious leader whose banner will confer the joys of martyrdom on those who fall. The Campaign of 1863 taught us to our cost that an expedition against the Fanatical Encampment may mean a war with a coalition of 53,000 fighting men[1] of the bravest races in the world. The inaccessible character of the country renders the temper and the internal relations of the tribes a matter of uncertainty with our Frontier officers; and whenever the Rebel Settlement suffers a defeat, it has merely to fall back deeper into the recesses of the Mahában.

On the 18th October 1863, a British Army of 7000 men,[2] under General Sir Neville Chamberlain, moved out with a train of artillery, and a supply at its command of 4000 mules and other beasts of burden, for which the whole Panjáb had been ransacked. Next evening a Column entered, by a night march, the defile overgrown with brushwood and overhung by trees, disastrously known as the Ambeyla Pass. Our base of operations was held by a strong cordon of troops,[3] and behind these

[1] I give the number of fighting men which each tribe can, without difficulty, turn out: — Husainzáis, 2000; Akazáis, 1000; Chigazáis, 6000; Madakhail, 4000; Amazáis, 1500; Jadúns, 4000; Khudákhail, 2000; Bonairs, 12,000; Bajaurs, 3000; Ranizáis, 2000; Dher Clan, 6000; Swát tribes, 10,000—Total, 53,500. I have taken these numbers from the Foreign Office Records, verified as far as possible by reference to Colonel Macgregor, who is engaged in the Frontier Gazetteer. The actual number in the field against us in 1863 rose at one time to 60,000.

[2] Infantry, Regulars, 5150; Cavalry, Regulars, 200; Artillery, 280; above 1000 Irregulars under the Civil Commissioner, and 13 guns.

[3] At Darband, 350 European Infantry, 250 Native Infantry, and 3 guns.

were the heavily-garrisoned Frontier Stations,[1] filled with Cavalry, Infantry, and Artillery. It was fortunate that the invading force was thus supported; for on the 20th the General found that the tribes whom he had considered friendly were wavering, and two days afterwards he telegraphed to Government that the force had had to come to a halt before getting out of the Pass. On the 23d the opposition of the tribes declared itself. The Bonairs attacked a reconnoitering party, and a few days later the Spiritual Head of the Swát Principality[2] threw in his lot with the enemy. Meanwhile, telegram after telegram reached the Government from the Frontier, begging for more and yet more troops. Our army had got locked up in a perilous defile. A wing of the Firozpur Regiment was ordered to the Frontier. Another Regiment of Infantry had to be hurried westwards from Pesháwar. The 93d Highlanders advanced by forced marches from Sialkot, and the 23d and 24th Native Infantry from Lahor. Before three weeks were over, the Panjáb Stations had been so denuded of troops, that

At Torbelá, one squadron of Native Cavalry, and details of Native Infantry. At Topi, 150 Native Cavalry, 250 Native Infantry, and 2 guns. At Abbottabad, one company of the 93d Highlanders, depots of the 5th Gurkhás and 1st Panjáb Infantry, 50 Native Cavalry, and 3 guns. At Rustam Bázár, 300 Native Cavalry, and details of Native Infantry. At Mardan, a depot of the Guide Corps.

[1] At Pesháwar, besides several batteries of Artillery, there were 1 Regiment of Hussars, 1 Regiment of European Infantry, 2 Regiments of Bengal Cavalry, and 3 Regiments of Native Infantry—the last weak in effective men, and having to hold outposts, which took up one Regiment. At Ráwal Pindí, 1 Regiment of Native Infantry, out of which 120 men were at Marí; 1 Battery of Artillery, one company of the 93d Highlanders, and depots of the 51st and 101st. At Kohát, 2 guns, 2 squadrons Native Cavalry, and 2 Regiments Panjáb Infantry, but weak. At Bannú, 2 guns, 1 Regiment Panjáb Cavalry, and 1 Regiment Panjáb Infantry. At Derá Ismá'íl Khán, 2 guns, 1 Regiment Panjáb Cavalry, and 1 Regiment Panjáb Infantry.

[2] An ascetic chief named Abd-ul-ghafúr, who had long exercised a superstitious ascendency over the Yusafzáí clans, and who is regarded with reverence by the Patháu tribes in general.

the officer commanding at Mianmir could with difficulty supply a guard of twenty-four bayonets for the Lieutenant-Governor.

Meanwhile the tribes were closing in upon our little Army. To advance was impossible; to move backward would have been worse than defeat. Our position gave every advantage to clans trained from boyhood in mountain war; and the following extract from the Journal of an officer, gives a fair idea of the disasters to which our troops were exposed:—

'The 20th, after recalling their outlying parties, retired, fighting the whole way into Camp, which they did not reach till long after dark. The enemy were in some strength, and tried to force their way into the lines; but by this time every one was ready for them, and they were met by a sharp file-fire from the Enfield rifles, and grape from the mountain-train guns. The night attack formed a curious and picturesque scene; the dark line of the jungle to the front; on the right and left the two port-fires of the mountain-train shining like stars, whilst between them a dim line of Infantry stretched across the valley. Suddenly comes a wild shout of Allah! Allah! the matchlocks flash and crack from the shadows of the trees; there is a glitter of whirling sword-blades, and a mob of dusky figures rush across the open space, and charge almost up to the bayonets. Then comes a flash and a roar, the grape and canister dash up the stones and gravel, and patter amongst the leaves at close range. The whole line lits up with the fitful flashes of a sharp file-fire, and as the smoke clears off, the assailants are nowhere to be seen; feeble groans from the front, and cries for water in some Pathán *patois*, alone tell us that the fire has been effectual. Presently comes another shot or two in a new direction. A few rolling stones on the hill inform the quick ears of the native troops that the enemy is attempting to take us in flank, and they push up to meet them at once: and so the line of fire, and sharp cracking of our rifles, extends gradually far up the dark and precipitous hill-side; and the roar of battle, multiplied a thousand-fold by the echoes of the mountain, fills the long valley from end to end. Then there is another shout and charge, more grape and musketry, which end as before. But this time a dark group, which moves slowly through our line, and carries tenderly some heavy burden, tells us that *their* shooting too has told.

'Presently from near the centre of the line comes a voice so full of command, that all stop to listen and prepare to obey. The order is, "Cease firing; let them charge up to the bayonet, and then"— The rest is lost, but every soldier knows well how the sentence ended, and stays his hand, waiting in deep silence, which contrasts strangely with the previous uproar. High up on a little knoll well to the front we see the tall form of the General towering above his staff, and looking intently into the darkness before him. Apparently, however, they had had enough, and but a few straggling shots from time to time told that an enemy, of whose numbers we could form no idea, still lay in the jungle before us. Presently these also ceased; but long afterwards we could hear their footsteps, and the stones rolling on the hills as they retired, and judged that they must be carrying off their dead and wounded, or they would have moved more quietly.'[1]

Every day's delay encouraged the hopes and strength-

[1] *Calcutta Review*, vol. lxxix. p. 201.

ened the fanatical zeal of the enemy. In spite of the reinforcements, our General found it impossible to advance. The British Army lay for weeks, to all appearance cowed within the Pass, not daring to emerge into the Chumlá Valley. Meanwhile the enemy, now swollen with the Bajaur tribes, threatened us simultaneously in front; upon our left flank; and on our rear communications. The Panjáb Government anxiously inquired on the 8th November, if the General, on receiving a reinforcement of 1600 Infantry, would advance to destroy the Fanatic Colony at Malká. On the 12th the answer came that 2000 more Infantry and some guns would be needed in order to render any forward movement practicable, and with the dispiriting intimation that the General deprecated any advance on Malká until the intermediate tribes could be brought to terms.

The whole Frontier was now in a flame. On the 4th November the Panjáb Government had found its military line so dangerously stripped of troops, that it borrowed a part of the escort belonging to the Viceroy's Camp, and hurried forward the 7th Fusiliers to the Frontier. A strong body of military police, horse and foot, were also sent to protect the rear communications, which the enemy had threatened. For the transport equipage, 4200 camels and 2100 mules were pressed in hot haste, and at an enormous cost, from our Panjáb Districts.[1] By the 14th November things had assumed a still more serious aspect, and the Commander-in-Chief of the British Forces in India hurried up to Lahor, and assumed the direction himself.

The truth is, that the Plan of the Campaign had completely failed. The original idea was, by a sudden

[1] Panjáb Government Letter of 18th February 1864, para. 67.

march through the Pass to occupy the open Valley beyond.[1] The Imperial Government had ordered that the whole operations should be completed by the 15th November. On the 14th, however, our Army still found it impossible to get out of the defile; and instead of a series of operations in an open valley, where the resources of civilised war could come into play, we had to undertake the defence of a very extended position in the hills. On the same day the Panjáb Government begged that an additional Brigade of 1500 men might be sent to the Frontier; and on the 19th, a telegram from General Chamberlain gave rise to most serious apprehensions as to whether the reinforcements would not arrive too late. On the 18th the enemy had attacked us in force, taking one of our pickets, and driving us back with a loss of 114 men, killed and wounded, besides officers. Next day the enemy again captured a picket, subsequently retaken after a bloody struggle, in which our General was himself dangerously hit, and 128 men, besides officers, left killed or *hors de combat.* On the 20th the sick and wounded, whom it had become absolutely necessary to send away, amounted to 425. The General's telegram of the 19th concluded as follows:—'The troops have now been hard worked both day and night for a month, and having to meet fresh enemies with loss is telling. We much need reinforcements. I find it difficult to meet the enemy's attacks and provide convoys for supplies and wounded sent to the rear. If you can give some fresh corps to relieve those most reduced in numbers and dash,

[1] Letter of the Panjáb Government, dated Lahor, 1st February 1864, para. 78. This document is the one which I have chiefly used for my account of the expedition. I can scarcely hope that the Narrative of so disastrous a campaign will escape hostile criticism, but I can only say that every statement I make is based upon the most carefully verified Official Reports.

the relieved corps can be sent to the plains and used in support. This is urgent.'

A great political catastrophe was now dreaded. Our Army, wearied out with daily attacks, might at any moment be seized with a panic, and driven back pell-mell, with immense slaughter, through the Pass. Such a misadventure, although costing fewer lives than a single great battle, would have ruined our prestige on the Frontier, and entailed political disasters, the end of which it was impossible to foretell. The Panjáb Government accordingly decided that, if General Chamberlain found it needful, the whole force should quietly retreat to Permauli. But the caution of the Panjáb Statesmen had underrated the unyielding persistence of British Troops. On the 22d came a telegram, stating that our Army was determined to hold its position, and that, although the difficulties were great, the General was sure of ultimate success.

Next day a wing of the 23d Native Infantry, with some European details, reached Camp. The enemy had already put forth his utmost strength, and the arrival of our fresh troops struck the tribes with an undefined terror. They began to realise what it is to be engaged against the inexhaustible resources of a vast Military Empire, and the next Friday (the day of the week which the Fanatics generally chose for battle) passed without an attack. Still we were unable to advance; and on the 28th November the Panjáb Government in vain recorded a Minute, deploring the stationary attitude of the force, and urging some forward movement. As our reinforcements arrived, fresh tribes poured down from the mountains, one chieftain[1] alone bringing in

[1] Faiztalal Khán of Bajaur.

3000 men, and a single ascetic[1] contributing 500 Fanatics determined upon martyrdom or victory.

On the 5th December our whole reinforcements had arrived, and an advance was again strongly urged. We had now 9000 Regular Troops, including several picked regiments, such as the 93d Highlanders, besides Irregulars; and it seemed hard to believe that a powerful British Army could thus remain cooped within the Pass week after week, harassed by the attacks of the enemy, and unable to strike a blow. But we had altogether underrated the hold which the Fanatical Colony possessed over the Frontier tribes. Those who joined them for the sake of the Faith burned with the hopes of plunder or of martyrdom, while the less bigoted clans were worked upon by the fear of their territory being invaded by the British or made the seat of the War. The clansmen, fired by zeal and rivalry, scorned all the efforts of a civilised Army, and an eye-witness thus describes the Frontier in the second week of December:—'The excitement was spreading far and wide. The Mahmands on the Pesháwar border were beginning to make hostile demonstrations at Shabkadr for the first time since their signal defeat near the same place in 1852 by the late Lord Clyde. Rumours were also reaching me from Kohát of expected raids by the Waziris and the Atmankhail; emissaries from Cabul and Jellalabad were with the Akhund (the Spiritual Head of the Swát tribes), who had also been further reinforced by Ghazan Khán, the Chief of Dher, and 6000 men. On the 5th December the Mahmands made a raid into our territory near Shabkadr.'[2]

But a coalition of mountain tribes is always capri-

[1] The Hájj, or Pilgrim, of Kunhar.

[2] Major James, Commissioner of the Pesháwar Division.

cious; and what our arms had failed to accomplish, dissensions and diplomacy began to effect. As early as the 25th November, the Commissioner of Pesháwar succeeded in drawing off certain clans of the Bonairs. Another contingent, to the number of 2000, he induced to return to their homes, and persuaded the Swát leader to disperse his immediate followers. Several minor chiefs, scenting the defection, withdrew, leaving the seeds of mutual distrust among those who remained. By the 10th December this distrust seemed ready to bear fruit. The great council of the Bonair Tribes suddenly came in to the Commissioner, but failed to arrange terms. On the 15th we hastened their deliberations by a night attack on Lalu, the enemy losing 400 men. On the 16th we burned the village of Ambeyla, and left 200 of the clansmen dead or wounded on the field. Before next day the Bonair tribes had made up their minds, and presenting themselves before the Commissioner, asked for orders. This defection proved the death-blow to the Fanatic cause. Every moment, some clan or another took itself off. The people from Bajaur and Dher fled. The whole of the Swát troops held themselves in instant readiness to desert. The coalition dissolved like a mountain mist, and the Bonair tribes, on whom the Rebel Settlement had chiefly depended, entered into an engagement with us to burn the Fanatics in their den. In less than a week a strong British brigade, reinforced and guided by the Bonairs, advanced in perfect safety through the mountains to the Fanatical Settlement at Malká, and reduced it to ashes. The force returned to the ill-fated Ambeyla Pass on the 23d December, and on the 25th the whole Army once more reached the plains, not a shot being fired on its homeward march.

Meanwhile we had left the fatal Defile thickly planted with the graves of British soldiers. Our loss amounted to no less than 847 men killed and wounded, or close on one-tenth of the total strength of the Army when it was eventually raised to 9000 Regular Troops. This was in the Pass alone, and irrespective of men invalided from exposure or who died of disease. The Panjáb Government, in summing up the results of the Campaign, declared that 'on no former occasion has the fighting in the hills been of so severe or sustained a character.' That the Fanatics had effected a formidable combination of tribes, and that in this coalition their Councils had maintained the ascendency. That these fanatics 'were no harmless or powerless religionists; that they are a permanent source of danger to our Rule in India; and that the Religious War which they have so persistently preached might have been adopted by all the Frontier tribes.' The peril of the crisis was augmented by the fact that just at that time the Indian Empire was without a responsible head. The Viceroy, Lord Elgin, lay in a dying state far in the interior of the hills, cut off from telegraphic communication, and unable to transact business.

Although the Campaign had cost us dear, it effectually quieted the border for the next four years. One half of the Fanatics had fallen, and the adjacent tribes were little inclined to view with favour the remnants of a Rebel Colony which had brought the tempest of War into their mountain valleys. The Traitor Chiefs felt themselves so unsafe, that in 1866 two of them[1] attempted to open a communication with our Frontier

[1] Muhammad Ishák and Muhammad Yakúb, through the instrumentality of Sayyid Mahmúd, formerly in our service.

officers. These efforts were frustrated by a third leader,[1] who now began to revive their zeal. Till the end of 1867, however, they were too busy with their own quarrels to venture upon depredations on our territory. But in February 1868 they moved out in a column of 700 fighting men, and tried to lay the foundation of a coalition of the clans. The remembrance of the punishment we had inflicted in 1863 made such an operation now more difficult. Still by degrees the superstitious fanaticism of the tribes began to get the better of their prudence. They attacked one of our outposts in the Agror Valley, and the Government recorded that, but for the immediate measures which we took, we should again have had to deal with a great tribal confederacy. This time, however, the British authorities were determined to lose not a moment. On the 8th September, the Supreme Government sanctioned the despatch of a military force to reduce the tribes. On the 30th October our troops moved out under the direction of the Commander-in-Chief in India, and the immediate command of General Wilde, C.B. At the same time we issued proclamations to the clans, reciting how certain tribes 'who had in no respect been interfered with or oppressed, after attacking a British outpost, entered our territory with arms and flags, burning sundry villages, and rendering retribution imperative;' 'The British Government, which is a long-suffering one, can bear with you no further, and calls you to account for the above acts.'

I do not propose to detail the events of this campaign. During July, urgent telegraphic messages had come from the Panjáb Government giving notice of the storm. 'The warning was so urgent,' wrote the Quarter-

[1] Maulaví Abd-ullah.

Master-General of the Army,[1] 'and the call for assistance so imperative, certain detachments of our troops being in fact beleaguered by the insurgents, that the Government of India lost no time.' Taught by the disasters of 1863, the Commander-in-Chief, instead of weakening the Panjáb Military Stations, or drawing detachments from our posts along the border, brought up regiments from the North-Western Provinces. Besides the operating column, numbering between 6000 and 7000 Regular Troops, the whole force on the Frontier was nearly doubled, and the flower of the British Army in India was concentrated against the fanatical mountain tribes.[2] During the suffocating heat of a tropical August and September, our soldiers were making forced marches such as have seldom been equalled in the healthy temperate zone. The Sappers and Miners, for example, covered six hundred miles in twenty-nine days. The troops poured northward from the inland Provinces in such bewildering masses as to completely overawe the clans, and to baffle the Fanatics' plan for a tribal coalition. At an enormous cost we placed an Army with Artillery complete on the Black Mountain, but the bor-

[1] Letter to Secretary to Government, Military Department, No. 163, dated 5th November 1868, para. 4.

[2] The D Battery F Brigade Royal Artillery, the E Battery 19th Brigade R.A., and the 2–24th Brigade R.A.; the 1st Battalions of the 6th and 19th Foot; 2 Companies of the 77th; the 16th Bengal Cavalry, the 2d Gurkhá Regiment; and the 24th Native Infantry, were at once transferred from Ráwal Pindí to Abbottabad, the Headquarters of the Hazára District. The 20th N.I. were marched from Lahor to Abbottabad; the 38th Foot from Sialkot to Darband in Hazára, which was also occupied by the 31st N.I. during the Campaign. The 1st and 4th Gurkhás were moved from the distant hill stations of Bakloh and Dharmsálá, and joined the force under General Wilde. In addition to the above, the 30th, 19th, and 23d N.I., the 9th Bengal Cavalry, and the 20th Hussars, were marched from their several stations of Cawnpur, Aligarh, Amritsar, Lahor, and Campbellpur, to Ráwal Pindí, and formed the reserve. Troops were also held in readiness at Pesháwar and Naushira to support the Guide Corps at Hot Mardan, opposite the Swát country.

derers did not dare to face it. 'The spectacle has been seen,' wrote the Quarter-Master-General, 'of British troops, European and Native, operating over and among mountains 10,000 feet high, the General in command himself being without a tent.'[1] Nevertheless we failed to reach the heart of the evil. It is doubtful how far religion was directly and immediately responsible for the rising. But the Panjáb Government, in summing up the results of the Campaign, recorded its regret that it 'had come to a close without our having been able either to drive out the Hindustání fanatics, or to induce them to surrender and to return to their homes in Hindustán.'[2]

I have now traced the history of the Rebel Camp on our Frontier from its formation in 1831 to the last Campaign in which it involved us in 1868. To trace the Wahábi warlike ramifications throughout India, would swell this little book to a great volume. But they were by no means confined to the Panjáb. For example, about thirty years ago, it seemed as if a Fanatic Confederacy had firmly established itself in the heart of Southern India. Sir Bartle Frere informs me that the Wahábi organisation of that day included a brother of the Nizám, who was to have been raised to the Haidrábád throne; and had the plan not broken through, the leaders would have had a great store of newly cast cannon and munitions of all sorts, with a formidable body of adherents, both among the semi-independent native Chiefs, and in the Military Courts of the South. The chronic miseries

[1] Letter from Quarter-Master-General to Secretary to Government, Military Department, No. 163, dated 5th November 1868, para. 17.

[2] Para. 22 of Panjáb Government's Letter, No. 258, dated 6th November 1868. In the above brief account of the Frontier Expedition of 1868, I have followed this letter and the reports from the local officers alluded to in it; with the Quarter-Master-General's letter of the 5th November 1868, and the Reports appended, for the military details.

which it rained down upon the border under the Sikh Rule, have been transmitted as a bitter legacy to ourselves. Besides constantly keeping alive a fanatical spirit of unrest along the Frontier, it has three times organised great tribal confederacies, each of which has cost British India a war. One Government after another has declared it to be a source of permanent danger to our Rule, yet all our efforts to extirpate it have failed. It still continues the centre towards which the hopes alike of our disloyal subjects and of our enemies beyond the Frontier turn. We know not at what moment we may again get involved in the dynastic struggles which constantly afflict Central Asia, but at present it seems quite possible that before this year ends we shall find ourselves in another Afghán War. When such a war arrives—and sooner or later it must come to pass—the Rebel Colony on our borders will be worth to the enemy many thousands of men. It is not the traitors themselves whom we have to fear, but the seditious masses in the heart of our Empire, and the superstitious tribes on our Frontier, both of whom the Fanatics have again and again combined in a Religious War against us. During nine centuries the Indian people have been accustomed to look for invasion from the north; and no one can predict the proportions to which this Rebel Camp, backed by the Musalmán hordes from the Westward, might attain, under a leader who knew how to weld together the nations of Asia in a Crescentade.

## CHAPTER II.

### THE CHRONIC CONSPIRACY WITHIN OUR TERRITORY.

THE source from which the Frontier Rebel Camp derived this extraordinary vitality long remained a mystery. Thrice it was scattered by the Native Power which preceded us in the Panjáb, and thrice it has been crushed beneath masses of British Troops. Yet it still lives on, and the devout Musalmáns find in this almost miraculous indestructibility a visible augury of ultimate triumph. The truth is, that while we have been trying to stamp out the Frontier Settlement beneath the heel of a military force, the fanatical sects among our Muhammadan subjects have been feeding it with an inexhaustible supply of money and men; pouring oil upon the embers which we had left for dead, and nursing them again into a flame.

The preaching of Sayyid Ahmad in 1820–22 passed unheeded by the British Authorities. He traversed our Provinces with a retinue of devoted disciples, converted the populace by thousands to his doctrine, and established a regular system of Ecclesiastical Taxation, Civil Government, and Apostolic Succession. Meanwhile our officers collected the revenue, administered justice, and paraded our troops, altogether unsuspicious of the great religious movement which was surging around them. From this unconsciousness they were in 1831 rudely awakened. Among the disciples of the Prophet in Calcutta, was a certain professional wrestler and bully, by name Titu Miyán.[1] This man had started life as the son of a respectable husbandman, and bettered his position by marrying into the family of a small landholder. But his violent and turbulent disposition threw away these advantages. For some time he earned an ignominious livelihood as a boxer in Calcutta, and afterwards enlisted in one of the bands of club-men with which the country gentlemen of Bengal were at that time wont to adjust their family differences and boundary disputes. This occupation finally landed him in jail. After his release he made a pilgrimage to Mecca, met Sayyid Ahmad in the Holy City, and returned to India a powerful preacher of the faith. He itinerated in the Districts north and east of Calcutta, making multitudes of converts, and preparing in secret God's vengeance against the Infidel. The Capture of Pesháwar in 1830 by the Fanatic Host emboldened Titu Miyán to throw off all disguise; and the petty oppressions[2] to which the Hindu landholders subjected his followers, placed him at the head of an infuriated peasant rising.

A series of agrarian outrages followed, ending in the insurgents entrenching themselves in a fortified Camp, and defying and beating back the English Authorities with some slaughter. The whole of the country north and east of Calcutta, including three entire Districts,[3] lay

[1] *Alias* Nisar Ali, a native of Chándpur Village, and resident in Barasat. His career is given at some length in the *Calcutta Review* vol. ci., which I have used along with an Official Memorandum by the Patna Magistrate.

[2] For example, Krishna Chandra Rai, a large landholder on the banks of the Ichhámati, levied a capitation tax of five shillings on each of his peasants who had embraced the new faith. Another proprietor threw one of his peasants into his private prison for destroying a shrine during the Muharram.

[3] The 24 Parganás, Naddea, and Faridpur.

at the mercy of insurgent bands between three and four thousand strong. The sectaries began by sacking a village in open daylight, because one of the inhabitants refused to accept their divine mission.[1] In another District a second village[2] was plundered, and a mosque burnt down. Meanwhile contributions of money and rice were levied from the Faithful; and on the 23d October 1831, the insurgents picked out a strongly situated village for their Headquarters, and erected a bamboo stockade round it. On the 6th November they marched out to the number of 500 fighting men, attacked a small town, and after murdering the priest, slaughtered two cows (the sacred animals of the Hindus), with whose blood they defiled a Hindu temple, and whose carcases they scoffingly hung up before the idol. They then proclaimed the extinction of the English Rule, and the re-establishment of the Muhammadan Power. Incessant outrages followed, the general proceeding being to kill a cow in a Hindu village, and, if the people resisted, to murder or expel the inhabitants, plunder their houses, and burn them down. They were equally bitter, however, against any Muhammadan who would not join their sect, and on one occasion, in sacking the house of a wealthy and obdurate Musalmán, varied the proceedings by forcibly marrying his daughter to the head of their band.

After some ineffectual efforts by the District Authorities, a detachment of the Calcutta Militia was sent out on the 14th November 1831 against the rebels. The fanatics, however, refused all parley, and the officer in command, being anxious to save bloodshed, ordered his men to load with blank cartridge. The insurgents poured out upon us, received a harmless volley, and instantly

[1] In Faridpur District. [2] At Sarfarázpúr, in Naddea.

cut our soldiers to pieces. All this took place within a couple of hours' ride from Calcutta. On the 17th the Magistrate got together some reinforcements, the Europeans being mounted on elephants. But the insurgents met them, drawn up in battle array a thousand strong, and chased the party to its boats on the river cutting down those who were slowest in the retreat. It now became necessary to deal with the rebels by means of Regular troops. A body of Native Infantry, with some Horse Artillery, and a detachment from the Body Guard, hurried out from Calcutta. The insurgents, disdaining the safety of their stockade, met the troops upon the open plain, 'with the mangled remains of a European, who had been killed the previous day, suspended in front of their line.' A stubborn engagement decided their fate. They were driven back pell-mell into their entrenchment, and the fortified camp was taken by storm. Titu Miyán, the leader, fell in the action. Of the survivors (350 in number), 140 were sentenced by the Court to various terms of imprisonment; and one of them, Titu's lieutenant, was condemned to death.

The end of the Reformers seemed to have come. On the Panjáb Frontier their forces had been scattered and their leader slain. The insurrection in Lower Bengal had met with a similar fate. But the Khalífs, or Apostolic Successors, whom the Prophet had appointed at Patna, came to the rescue. They produced eye-witnesses, who declared that in the thick of the battle the Prophet had been snatched away from mortal sight in a cloud of dust. They assured the multitude that he had himself foretold his disappearance. The Prophet had indeed prayed that his grave might be hidden from his disciples, like that of Moses of old, so that no impious worship might be paid to his bones. They preached that the Almighty had withdrawn him from a faint-hearted generation; but that when the Indian Musalmáns, with singleness of mind, should join in a Holy War against the English Infidels, their Prophet would return and lead them to victory. In all this there was nothing incredible to a Musalmán. 'Such things had happened before. It was well known that the Prophet Yunis (Jonah) had disappeared for a time, and lay concealed in the belly of a large fish. Moses, too, became invisible when he ascended Mount Sinai to receive the Old Testament. Zulkarnain, the great leader who imprisoned Gog and Magog, disappeared under similar circumstances. The Prophet Christ had not tasted of death.'[1] It was therefore incumbent on the Faithful to re-enter on the Holy War with fresh vigour; and the Khalífs at Patna appointed a new General of the Faith,[2] who moved northwards with an ever-growing retinue of fanatic swordsmen.

For a time the well-attested miracle of the Prophet's Apotheosis overawed inquiry, and all went well. One of the most devoted of the Lower Bengal missionaries, who had preached 'throughout the Eastern Districts, particularly in Dacca and Sylhet,' marched northwards 1800 miles to the Frontier with a thousand men. But the protracted absence of the Prophet greatly exercised his faith, and after a short campaign he resolved to penetrate to the distant mountain-cave in which the Lord had hidden his Apostle. His zeal for the truth surmounted the watchful jealousy of the more interested party leaders; and having reached the hill sanctuary, he found in it 'only three figures stuffed with straw.' The dis-illusioned missionary fled from the accursed den, commanded his

[1] *Calcutta Review*, vol. ci. p. 187. [2] Maulaví Nasr-ud-dín.

followers to return to their homes, and indited a long indignant letter to his converts in Calcutta, who still kept forwarding money and men.

'*Salám 'alaikum,*' he wrote, 'the peace and blessing of God be upon you. Mulla Kádir prepared an image of the Prophet, but before showing it to any person he made the people promise that they would never attempt to shake hands with the Prophet or speak to him; for if they did, then the Prophet would disappear for fourteen years. The whole people, deeply affected, viewed this lifeless image from some distance, and made obeisance to it. But to all their supplications never an answer came, and the people grew desirous of shaking hands with their Prophet. Then Mulla Kádir tried to allay their suspicions, and said that if any one should attempt to shake hands with the Prophet without giving previous notice, the Prophet's servant would pistol him.' The letter goes on to relate how the astute Mulla reproached the people with their want of faith; how the image was removed from public view; and finally, how, 'after a great deal of entreaty, they obtained an inspection of it. They examined it, and found that it was a goat's skin stuffed with grass, which, with the help of some pieces of wood and hair, was made to resemble a man. Your slave inquired of the priest about this. He answered that it was true, but that the Prophet had performed a miracle and appeared as a stuffed figure to the people. The errors and falsity of these impostors are now as clear as noonday, and I have saved my soul from sin.'

Again the fanatic cause seemed ruined. But the missionary zeal of the Patna Khalífs, and the immense pecuniary resources at their command, once more raised the sacred banner from the dust. They covered India with their emissaries, and brought about one of the greatest religious revivals that has ever taken place. The two Khalífs[1] themselves went through Bengal and Southern India. The minor missionaries were innumerable, and a skilful organisation enabled them to settle in any place where the multitude of converts made it worth their while. In this way, almost every one of the fanatic Districts had its permanent preacher, whose zeal was sharpened from time to time by visits of the itinerant missionaries, and whose influence was consolidated and rendered permanent by the Central Propaganda at Patna. How great a power for evil these preachers have now become in Bengal, I shall afterwards show. In Southern India they raised such a hurricane of enthusiasm, that even the women cast their jewels into the common purse. From the North-West Provinces they sent company after company of recruits to the Fanatic Camp. Everywhere they stirred the Muhammadan population to its depths; and although the keen intellect of the Bengáli eventually gave its present tone to the movement, the revival burst forth with equal heat for a time in all the Provinces of India. 'They have,' wrote the Magistrate of Patna, 'under the very nose and protection of Government authorities, openly preached sedition in every village of our most populous districts, unsettling the minds of the Musalmán population, and

[1] Wiláyat Alí and Ináyat Alí. The former, after a missionary tour through Bengal, took Bombay, the Nizámat, and Central India as his special field. Ináyat concentrated his efforts on the Middle Districts of the Lower Provinces, Malda, Bogra, Rájsháhí, Patna, Naddea, and Faridpur. Karámat Alí of Jaunpur carried the movement eastwards from Faridpur into Dacca, Maimansingh, Noakhali, and Barisal. Zain-ul-'Abidín, a native of Haidrábád, who had been converted by Wiláyat Alí on his tour through Southern India, selected North-eastern Bengal as the sphere of his labours, and converted the peasantry of N. Tipperah and Sylhet.—*Calcutta Review*, vols. c. and ci.

obtaining an influence for evil as extraordinary as it is certain.'[1]

The origin of this wonderful influence was, however, by no means based on unmixed evil. Sayyid Ahmad commenced his apostolic career by re-asserting the two great principles with which all true preachers have worked—the unity of God and the equality of man. He appealed with an almost inspired confidence to the religious instinct, long dormant in the souls of his countrymen, and overgrown by the superstitious accretions with which centuries of contact with Hinduism had almost stifled Islám. He found the True Faith buried beneath the ceremonial of idolatry. Bandit as he had been, impostor as he or his immediate disciples became, I cannot help the conviction that there was an intermediate time in Sayyid Ahmad's life when his whole soul yearned with a great pain for the salvation of his countrymen, and when his heart turned singly to God. A man of an intensely nervous temperament, concealed under an outward show of calm, he fell into religious trances which to Western science would simply suggest epilepsy, but which the popular belief of Asia reverences as a state of direct communion with the Almighty. In unearthly ecstasies the Prophets of bygone ages flitted before his inner vision, and he held a constant mystic intercourse with the long-dead founders of the two great Religious Orders of India. In 1820, when he started on his mission, he was about thirty-four years old, a little above the middle height, and with a long beard falling on his breast. Of a taciturn, gentle manner, unlearned in the law, he preached on the practical life of his countrymen, and abstained from all doctrinal discussions; either, as his enemies said, because he was

[1] Official Proceedings, 1865.

unfit to handle them; or, as his disciples affirmed, because they were below his high order of piety. Two of his first converts were men of profound scholarship, brought up at the feet of the Dehli sage, 'The Sun of India,' under whom the Prophet also passed his noviciate.

These two men[1] belonged to the family of the greatest Muhammadan Doctor of the age, and had been carefully trained by him alike in the sacred language and in the Sacred Law. Both of them were imbued, although in different degrees, with the necessity of a reformation of the faith and manners of their countrymen; and both simultaneously accepted their illiterate co-disciple, the late bandit, as a man sent by God to accomplish the work. The veneration with which these learned and polished doctors of the law publicly treated the ignorant horse-soldier, with his late-learned smattering of Arabic, first attracted popular attention to the future Prophet. Their profound acquaintance with the patristic literature of Islám enabled them publicly to support the Sayyid's title, which they themselves had acknowledged. Starting with the popular belief that God from time to time sends Imáms, or leaders, to quicken the faith of His children, and to guide the masses of mankind to salvation, they proved that Sayyid Ahmad had all the marks of such a divinely commissioned envoy. He was, in the first place, lineally descended in the orthodox line from Muhammad himself. In his fits of religious ecstasy, during which he communed with God and the Apostles; in his grave, taciturn, and gentle demeanour; even in his person, they declared him to resemble the great Prophet. Of the twelve Khalífs who will reduce the world to the True

[1] Maulaví Muhammad Ismá'íl, the nephew, and Maulaví Abd-ul-haí, the son-in-law, of Sháh Abd-ul-azíz.

Faith, some of the Indian Muhammadans[1] believe that six have already come and gone, while others only admit four. Sayyid Ahmad was the next in the sacred line. In dreams, the beloved daughter of Muhammad and her husband (his lineal ancestors) visited him, saluted him as their son, bathed him in sweet essences, and arrayed him in royal apparel. What further evidence could the populace, or indeed even Sayyid Ahmad himself, demand? His own humility and scruples disappeared before the incessant arguments of his two learned disciples. So firmly did he at length believe in his title, that at the peril of his life he assumed all the functions of sovereignty, levied tithes, appointed Khalífs to continue the Apostolic Succession, and formally proclaimed himself at Pesháwar the Commander of the Faithful.

Until his pilgrimage to Mecca, however, he does not appear to have reduced his doctrines to any formulated system. His idea of a reformation of religion was a purely practical one. He told his hearers, that if they were to escape divine wrath, they must live better lives. One of his disciples has recorded his sayings in a book,[2] now the Kurán of the sect; in which, however, the brief utterances of the Prophet are believed to have been greatly amplified by the piety of the writer. But even when thus amplified, his teaching seems to have been almost entirely one of practical morality. In the Deeds by which he appointed the Patna Khalífs, the same spirit of the religion of daily life shines out. His single doctrine was to worship God alone, and God direct, without the interposition of humanly devised forms and ceremonies.

[1] The Sunnis. The Shiahs hold that eleven have already passed away, and that the twelfth is hidden somewhere beyond our North-Western Frontier. But the Sunnis form 95 per cent. of the Indian Musalmáns.

[2] The Sirát-ul-Mustakím, by Muhammad Ismá'íl.

'In the name of the merciful God! Be it known to those who seek the way of God in general, and to those in particular, whether present or absent, who are the friends of Sayyid Ahmad, that the object of such as become disciples of holy men by the ceremony of joining hands is to secure the means of pleasing God, and depends on fulfilling the law of his Prophet.

'The law of the Prophet is founded on two things: First, the not attributing to any creature the attribute of God;[1] and second, not inventing forms and practices[2] which were not invented in the days of the Prophet, and his successors or Khalífs. The first consists in disbelieving that angels, spirits, spiritual guides, disciples, teachers, students, prophets or saints, remove one's difficulties. In abstaining from having recourse to any of the above creations for the attainment of any wish or desire. In denying that any of them has the power of granting favour or removing evils; in considering them as helpless and ignorant as one's self in respect to the power of God. In never making any offering to any prophet, saint, holy man, or angel for the obtaining of any object, but merely to consider them as the friends of God. To believe that they have power to rule the accidents of life, and that they are acquainted with the secret knowledge of God, is downright infidelity.[3]

'With regard to the second point, true and undefiled religion consists in strongly adhering to all the devotions and practices in the affairs of life which were observed in the time of the Prophet. In avoiding all such innovations as marriage ceremonies, mourning ceremonies, adorning of tombs, erection of large edifices over graves, lavish expenditure on the anniversaries of the dead, street pro-

[1] Shirk. [2] Bid'at. [3] Kufr.

cessions and the like, and in endeavouring as far as may be practicable to put a stop to these practices.'[1]

The Prophet's visit to Mecca in 1822–23 amplified and formulated this simple system of puritanic belief. He found the Holy City just emerged from a Reformation devised by a Bedouin of the desert, and similar in principles to his own. Its founder had erected a great religious empire in Western Asia, closely resembling that which Sayyid Ahmad hoped to establish in India. It becomes necessary, therefore, to break the narrative of the further development of his creed, by a brief account of the rise and progress of the Wahábis in Arabia.

About a hundred and fifty years ago, a young Arab pilgrim, by name Abd-ul-Wahháb,[2] the son of a petty Nejd chief, was deeply struck with the profligacy of his fellow-pilgrims, and with the endless mummeries which profaned the Holy Cities. For three years he pondered over the corruptions of Muhammadanism in Damascus, and then stepped forth as their denouncer. He rendered himself peculiarly hateful to the creatures of the Constantinople Court, accusing the Turkish Doctors of making the written word of no effect by their traditions (*Sunnát*), and the Turkish people of being worse than the Infidels by reason of their vices. Driven from city to city, he at length took refuge with the chief of Derai'yeh, Muhammad Ibn Sa'úd, into whom he instilled his religious views and a sense of his great wrongs. These wrongs he was soon amply to redress. With the aid of his new convert, who married his daughter, he formed a small Arab League, and raised the standard of revolt against the Government of Constantinople, and of protest against her

[1] *Calcutta Review*, No. c. p. 89.

[2] 'The Servant of Him who gives everything.'

corrupted creed. Victory crowded upon victory. The Bedouins, who had never adored Muhammad as quite a divine person, nor accepted the Kurán as an altogether inspired book, flocked to the Army of the Reformation. The greater part of Nejd was conquered, Abd-ul-Wahháb being the spiritual chief, while Muhammad Ibn Sa'úd, his son-in-law, ruled as its temporal monarch. They appointed governors for the vanquished provinces, and kept them in strict subjection. A great Assembly of the Sa'úd Tribe formed the Ministry for legislative and religious affairs during time of peace, and the Council of War during campaigns.

Before long the new Kingdom boldly attacked the Turkish power. In 1748 the Pasha of Bagdád, formerly Grand Vizier, had to take active measures against the movement,—a movement which would in the end have thrust out the degenerate successors of the Khalífs from the Porte, and constructed a new Muhammadan Empire. Nor were the Reformers less skilful in civil government than they had been victorious in arms. They bound together the Nomad Arabs, on whom their power chiefly depended, in a firm confederation. A regular system of religious taxation was devised. In time of war, four-fifths of the spoil went to soldiers, and one-fifth to the Royal Treasury. The Land-tax, termed Alms in the Kurán, was strictly enforced; fields watered naturally by rain or rivers paying one-tenth of the yearly produce, while land which required artificial irrigation paid one-twentieth. Traders of all sorts paid one and a half per cent. of their capital. Rebellious or schismatic cities and Provinces also yielded a steady source of Revenue. The punishment for a first defection was general plunder, one-fifth of which went to the treasury. In case of a second rebellion or apostasy, the whole land on which the town was built, with the territory immediately subject to it became the property of the Wahábi chief. As the Reformers were essentially a sect militant, and boldly announced the doctrine of conversion by the sword, this proved a valuable source of revenue, and was enforced by two or three campaigns every year.

The doctrines which they thus engraved in blood were themselves of a noble type. They insisted first of all upon a practical amendment of morals. The Turks had infected the Holy City itself with their low sensuality. Not content with polygamy, they had brought women of the vilest character with them in their pilgrim trains, and were addicted to practices of an even more filthy nature among themselves,—practices solemnly forbidden by the Kurán. Wine and opium they had openly used in the Holy Streets, and the Turkish caravan to Mecca exhibited a scene of the most abominable debauchery. It was against these practical and visible defilements that Abd-ul-Wahháb first raised his voice. But by degrees his views grew into a theological system which has been handed down under the name of Wahábi-ism,[1] and which is now substantially the belief of the Indian sect. It is a system which reduces the religion of Muhammad to a pure Theism, and consists of seven great doctrines. First, absolute reliance upon One God. Second, absolute renunciation of any mediatory agent between man and his Maker, including the rejection of the prayers of the saints, and even of the semi-divine mediation of Muhammad himself. Third, the right of private interpretation of the Muhammadan Scriptures, and the rejection of all priestly

[1] In Arabic, Wahábi is spelt *Wahhábí*, but it has now become an Anglo-Indian word. I accent the middle syllable to show that it is long.

glosses on the Holy Writ. Fourth, absolute rejection of all the forms, ceremonies, and outward observances with which the mediæval and modern Muhammadans have overlaid the pure Faith. Fifth, constant looking for the Prophet (Imám), who will lead the True Believers to victory over the Infidels. Sixth, constant recognition both in theory and practice of the obligation to wage war upon all Infidels. Seventh, implicit obedience to the spiritual guide. The Wahábis form, in fact, an advanced division of the Sunnis—the Puritans of Islám. The Sunnis are the sect to which almost all the Muhammadans of Bengal and the North-Western Provinces belong.[1]

Abd-ul-Wahháb died in 1787, but bequeathed his conquests to a worthy successor. In 1791 the Wahábis made a successful campaign against the grand Sheikh of Mecca. In 1797 they beat back the Pasha of Bagdád with immense slaughter, and overran the most fertile Provinces of Asiatic Turkey. In 1801 they again swept down upon Mecca with more than a hundred thousand men, and in 1803 the Holy City fell into their hands. Next year they captured Medina. In these two strongholds of Islám, the Reformers massacred the inhabitants who refused to accept their creed, plundered and defiled the tombs of the Muhammadan saints, and spared not even the Sacred Mosque itself. During eleven centuries every devout King and Emperor of Islám had sent thither

[1] They are chiefly Sunnis of the Hanafi persuasion, with, however, a few Sháfi'ís. The Hanafis follow the order of their great Imám, Abu Hanífa; born about 80 A.H. (699 A.D.); died about 115 A.H. (733 A.D.). They pray five times daily, and during prayer keep their hands crossed over the navel, bending the body forward, but not raising the hands above the head. After prayer they utter the word Amen in silence. The Sháfi'ís also take their name from their Imám, Abu Abd-ulláh Sháfi'; born about 150 A.H. (767 A.D); died about 204 A.H. (819–820 A.D.). They cross the hands over the breast at prayer, raise them above the head when they bow, and at the end utter Amen aloud.

the richest oblations which his realm could yield, and the accumulated offerings of the world's piety were now swept into the tents of the sectaries of the desert.

The consternation of the Muhammadan world can only be compared to the thrill which passed through Christendom, when it was told that Bourbon's banditti had bivouacked in the Vatican, and that the Vicar of Christ was a prisoner in Sant' Angelo. The highest temple of the Musalmán faith was not only pillaged, but grossly polluted by armed schismatics; the Prophet's own tomb was mutilated; and the path of pilgrimage, the Musalmán's avenue to salvation, was closed. From the marble pile of Saint Sophia in Constantinople, to the plastered wayside mosque on the frontier of China, every Muhammadan house of prayer was filled with lamentation and weeping. A few of the Shiahs declared it was the Twelfth Imám made manifest; but to the orthodox believer it seemed clear that Ad-Dajjál, the lying Prophet foretold by Muhammad, had now descended on the earth, and that the end was come.

Spite of fasting and supplication, from 1803 to 1809 no great pilgrim caravan crossed the desert. The Wahábis overran Syria, sustained a War with the British in the Persian Gulf, and threatened Constantinople itself. It was Mehemet Ali, Pasha of Egypt, who at last succeeded in crushing the Reformation. In 1812, Thomas Keith, a Scotchman, under the Pasha's son, took Medina by storm. Mecca fell in 1813; and five years later, this vast power, which had so miraculously sprung up, as miraculously vanished, like a shifting sand mountain of the desert.

The Wahábis, now a scattered and a homeless sect, profess doctrines hateful to the well-to-do classes of Muhammadans. In formal divinity they are the Unitarians of Islám. They refuse divine attributes to Muhammad, forbid prayers in his name, and denounce supplications to departed saints. It is their earnest, practical morality, however, that contains the secret of their strength. They boldly insist upon a return to the faith of the primitive Muhammadan Church, to its simplicity of manners, its purity of life, and its determination to spread the Truth, at whatever expense of the blood of the Infidel, and at whatever sacrifice of themselves. Their two great principles are the unity of God and the abnegation of self. They disdain the compromises by which the rude fanaticism of Muhammad has been skilfully worked up into a system of civil polity, and adapted alike to the internal wants and foreign relations of Musalmán States. They exact from every convert that absolute resignation (*islám*) to the will of God which is the clue to the success of Muhammad. But while, like other reforming sects, they ceaselessly insist on this fundamental doctrine, they weaken their cause among the learned by their unitarian divinity, and among the simple by a rude disregard of established rites and hallowed associations. In the greater part of Asia, the Wahábi convert must separate himself from the whole believing world. He must give up his most cherished legends, his most solemn festivals, his holiest beliefs. He must even discontinue the comforting practice of praying at his father's tomb.[1]

The Wahábis of India, however, appeal to a principle in the Muhammadan heart, whose intensity makes light of all these difficulties. While at Mecca, Sayyid Ahmad attracted the notice of the authorities by the similarity of

[1] Here and further on I have followed an article which I put forth in the *Indian Daily News* in 1864.

his teaching to that of the Bedouin Sectaries, from whom the Holy City had lately suffered so much. The priests publicly degraded him, and expelled him from the town. As a natural result of this persecution, he returned to India no longer a religious visionary and reformer of idolatrous abuses, but a fanatical disciple of Abd-ul-Wahháb. Whatever had been dreamy in his nature now gave place to a fiery ecstasy, in which he beheld himself planting the Crescent throughout every district of India, and the Cross buried beneath the carcases of the English Infidels. Whatever had been indistinct in his teaching, henceforth assumed the precision of that fierce, formulated theology, by which Abd-ul-Wahháb had founded a great Kingdom in Arabia, and which Sayyid Ahmad hoped would enable him to rear a still greater and more lasting Empire in India.

The internal change that took place in the Prophet's heart is known only to himself and to God, but it is certain that his whole outward conduct altered. He no longer looked upon making converts as his work in life, but only as a preliminary process to his entering on that work. At Bombay, where he first landed, not even the multitudes who flocked to his preaching, and begged for the initiatory rite, could delay him. Wherever he went, his success was even greater than before his visit to Mecca; but he seemed to view preaching in the settled Districts with a certain disdainful impatience, and to keep his eye constantly fixed upon the distant warlike populations of the Frontier. His subsequent career has been sufficiently described in the foregoing chapter. It remains briefly to explain the doctrinal system which his followers have evolved from his teaching; a system by which they effected one of the greatest religious revivals known to Indian history, and which has kept alive the spirit of revolt against the British Rule during fifty years.

The first difficulty that confronted the Indian Wahábis was the disappearance of their leader. His death had disappointed the hopes of his personally leading the Faithful to victory, and this untoward event had to be provided for in the new doctrine of the sect. All Muhammadans believe that the end of the world will be ushered in by wars and seditions, great social upheavals, the rise of low persons to high places, by earthquake, by pestilence and famine. In that latter time will come the Imám Mahdi, a descendant of Muhammad, and bearing his name, born beyond the north-west frontier of the Panjáb, hidden from the eyes of men during a part of his career, but finally the Ruler of Arabia and the conqueror of Constantinople, which, before then, will again have been subjected to a Christian King. Then Antichrist shall appear, and wage bitter war against the Imám. In the end, 'Christ will descend on earth near a white tower to the east of Damascus,' destroy the legions of the wicked one, and convert the whole world to the True Faith of Muhammad.

The Indian Wahábis had claimed for Sayyid Ahmad the title of the great Imám, who should thus precede the final coming of Christ. But the events amid which his career closed could in no way be reconciled with the popular conception of this last struggle between good and evil. They therefore boldly attacked the general belief, and asserted that the true Imám Mahdi was to come, not at the Last Day, but as an intermediate leader half-way between the death of Muhammad and the end of the world. They showed that he had all the *stigmata*, to borrow an analogy from Christian history, of the appointed

Imám. They brought an immense phalanx of authorities to prove that the 13th century of their era (1786–1886 A.D.) was the period in which the Imám Mahdi should appear. Ahmad was born in 1786. Even the Shiah Doctors, hateful as their doctrines were to the Reformers, were made use of. The Shiahs, indeed, had been much more exact than the Sunnis, and fixed his advent in 1260 A.H., or A.D. 1844. Had not Muhammad himself said, 'When you see the black flags coming from Khorassán, go forth, for with them is a Khalíf, the Envoy of God?' The subversion of India beneath the Christian power, and a hundred other signs of the times, plainly announced the time of tribulation which was to herald his advent. Prophecies were forged to give still greater certainty, of which the following verses, taken from a long poem still sung in Northern India, may serve as an example :—

'I see the power of God—I see distress in this world ;
On all sides I see great Armies fighting and plundering ;
I see low-born people learned in unprofitable learning, wearing the garb of the priesthood.
I see the decline of virtue, the increase of pride ;
I see disputes and wars between the Turks and Persians.
I see beautiful countries deserted by the pious, and become the abode of the wicked.
Though I see all this, I do not despair, as I see one the dispeller of Sorrow ;
I see that after 1200 years[1] have passed, wonderful events will occur ;
I see all the Kings of the earth arrayed one against the other ;
I see the Hindus in an evil state ; I see the Turks oppressed ;
Then the Imám will appear and rule over the earth ;
I see and read A.H.M.D.[2] (Ahmad), as the letters showing forth the name of this ruler.'

---

[1] The original poem gives 750, which was changed to suit Ahmad's death. *Calcutta Review*, vol. c. p. 100, from which I extract these verses.

[2] The original poem had M.H.M.D. (Muhammad).

Another favourite prophecy runs thus :—

THE ODE OF NI'MAT-ULLAH.[1]

*(May his grave be considered sacred.)*

'I tell the truth that there will be a King,
By the name of Timúr, and he will reign thirty years.'

*(Here follows a list of his successors down to the last of Sháh Jahán's family.)*

'Then there will be another King.
Nadir will invade Hindustán.
His sword will cause the massacre of Dehli.
After this, Ahmad Sháh will invade.
And he will destroy the former dynasty.
After the death of this King,
The descendants of the former King will be reinstated.
The Sikh tribe will grow powerful at this time, and commit all sorts of cruelties.
This will continue till forty years.
Then the Nazarenes will take all Hindustán.
They will reign a hundred years.
There will be great oppression in the world in their reign.
For their destruction there will be a King in the West.
This King will proclaim a war against the Nazarenes.
And in the war a great many people will be killed.
The King of the West will be victorious by the force of the sword in a Holy War,
And the followers of Jesus will be defeated.
Islám will prevail for forty years.
Then a faithless tribe will come out from Ispahán.
To drive out these tyrants, Jesus will come down, and the expected Mahdi will appear.
All these will occur at the end of the world.
In 570[2] Hijra, this ode is composed.
In 1270[3] the King of the West will appear.
Ni'mat-ullah knew the mysteries of God;
His prophecies will be fulfilled to men.'

Having established the divine mission of their leader, the Indian Wahábis passed direct from all minor questions to the great doctrine of Religious War. Throughout

[1] I select a few verses from the entire ode, given in the Official Record of the Wahábi Trial of 1865.

[2] 1174–1175 A.D.

[3] 1853–1854 A.D.

the whole literature of the sect, this obligation shines forth as the first duty of regenerate man. Their earliest work thus lays down the law:—'Holy War is a work of great profit: just as rain does good to mankind, beasts and plants, so all persons are partakers in the advantages of a War against the Infidel. The advantages are twofold: general, of which all men, even idolaters and infidels, animals and vegetables, partake; special, of which only certain classes are partakers, and partake in different degrees. In connection with the general advantages, it may be said that the blessings of Heaven,—viz. copious showers at seasonable times, abundant supplies of vegetable produce; good times, so that people are void of care and free from calamities, whilst their property increases in value; an increase in the number of learned men, in the justness of judges, in the conscientiousness of suitors, and in the liberality of the rich,—that these blessings, increased an hundred-fold, are granted when the dignity of the Muhammadan religion is upheld, and Muhammadan kings possessing powerful armies become exalted, and promulgate and enforce the Muhammadan law in all countries. But look at this country (India), as compared with Turkey or Turkistán, as far as the blessings of Heaven are concerned. Nay, compare the present state of Hindustán in this year 1233 Hijra (A.D. 1818), when the greater portion of it has become the Country of the Enemy (*dár-ul-harb*), with the state of India some two or three centuries back, and contrast the blessings of Heaven now vouchsafed and the number of learned men with those of that period.'

Their most popular song breathes the same spirit. The rebels in the Camp on our Frontier were drilled morning and evening to the sound of its solemn strains, and the companies of recruits who passed northwards from the heart of our territory chaunted its stanzas along the British high roads.

'First I glorify God, who is beyond all praise; I laud his Prophet, and write a song on Holy War:

Holy War is a War carried on for religion, without any lust of Power. In the Sacred Scriptures its glories are related: I mention a few.

War against the Infidel is incumbent on all Musalmáns; make provision for it before all things.

He who from his heart gives one farthing to the cause, shall hereafter receive seven hundred fold;

And he who both gives and joins in the fight, shall receive seven thousand fold from God.

He who shall equip a warrior in this cause of God shall obtain a martyr's reward;

His children dread not the trouble of the grave; nor the last trump; nor the Day of Judgment.

Cease to be cowards; join the divine leader, and smite the Infidel.

I give thanks to God that a great leader has been born in the thirteenth century of the Hijra.[1]

Oh friend, since you must some time die, is it not better to offer up your life in the service of the Lord?

Thousands go to war and come back unhurt; thousands remain at home and die.

You are filled with worldly care, and have forgotten your Maker in thinking of your wives and children.

How long will you be able to remain with your wives and children? how long to escape death?

If you give up this world for the sake of God, you enjoy the pleasures of Heaven for ever.

Fill the uttermost ends of India with Islám, so that no sounds may be heard but "Alláh! Alláh!"'[2]

But any attempt at even the briefest epitome of the Wahábi Treatises in prose and verse on the duty to wage war against the English would fill a volume. The sect has developed a copious literature filled with prophecies of the downfall of the British Power, and devoted to the duty of Religious Rebellion. The mere titles of its

[1] A.D. 1786–1886.

[2] Risála-Jihád, or Wahábi War Song. *Calcutta Review*, vol. cii. p. 396 *et seq.*

favourite works suffice to show their almost uniformly treasonable character. I give below[1] a list of thirteen. Some of them are of so flagrant a character as to require to be secretly passed from hand to hand in manuscript. Others are widely circulated. The poison, however, is not confined to their readers alone, but is carried into

[1] 1. Sirát-ul-Mustakím, or the Straight Path, being the sayings of the Prophet Sayyid Ahmad, the Amír-ul-Múminín (Leader of the Faithful). Written in Persian by Maulaví Muhammad Ismá'íl of Dehli; translated into Hindustáni by Maulaví Abd-ul-Jabbár of Cawnpur.

2. Kasída, or Book of Poetry, setting forth the obligation of waging war against the Infidel, and the rewards of all who partake in it, by Maulaví Karam Alí of Cawnpur.

3. Sharh-i-Wakáya, a treatise on War against the Infidel, with 'full instructions as to those by whom and with whom the fight is to be made.' This work, however, only insists upon a Holy War when the Infidel oppresses the True Believer.

4. A Prophetic Poem by Maulaví Ni'mat-ullah, foretelling the downfall of the British Power, and the coming of a King from the West who shall deliver the Indian Muhammadans from the English.

5. Tawáríkh Kaisar Rúm, or Misbáh-us-Sarí, being a history of Abd-ul-Wahháb, the Founder of the sect; his persecutions and wars against the Turkish apostates. MS.

6. Asár Mahshar, or Signs of the Last Day, by Maulaví Muhammad Alí, printed in 1265 A.H., or 1849 A.D. This book of Poetry has been widely circulated. It foretells a war in the Khyber hills on the Panjáb Frontier, where the English will first vanquish the Faithful, whereupon the Muhammadans will make search for their true Imám. Then there will be a battle lasting four days, ending in the complete overthrow of the English, 'even the very smell of Government being driven out of their heads and brains.' Thereafter the Imám Mahdi will appear; and the Muhammadans being now the rulers of India, will flock to meet him at Mecca. These events will be heralded in by an eclipse both of the sun and moon in the month of Ramazán.

7. The Takwiat-ul-Imán, or Strengthening of the Faith, written by Maulaví Muhammad Ismá'íl of Dehli.

8. Tazkír-ul-Akháwí, or Brotherly Conversation, by the same author.

9. Nasíhat-ul-Muslimín, or Advice to Muhammadans, by Maulaví Karam Alí of Cawnpur.

10. The Hidáyat-ul-Múminín, or Guide to the Faithful, written by Aulad Husain.

11. Tanwír-ul-Ainain, or Enlightening of the Eyes, an Arabic work.

12. Tanbíh-ul-Gháfilín, or Rebuke of the Negligent, in Urdu.

13. Chihil Hadís, or the forty traditions of Muhammad regarding Holy War.

every District of Bengal by a swarm of preachers, every one of whom is carefully nurtured in treason before he goes forth on his proselytising work.

Many of these works are openly sold in the towns of British India, the most violent and seditious finding the greatest favour with the multitude. But an inflammatory literature is only one part of a permanent fourfold organisation which the Wahábi leaders use for spreading the doctrine of Rebellion. Besides it they have, in the first place, the Central Propaganda at Patna, which for a time defied the British Authorities in that city, and which, although to a certain extent broken up by repeated State Trials, still exerts an influence throughout all Bengal. The Prophet, in appointing Khalífs at Patna in 1821, chose men of indomitable zeal and strength of will. We have seen how, time after time, when the cause appeared ruined, they again and again raised the standard of Holy War from the dust. Indefatigable as missionaries, careless of themselves, blameless in their lives, supremely devoted to the overthrow of the English Infidels, admirably skilful in organising a permanent system for supplying money and recruits, the Patna Khalífs stand forth as the types and exemplars of the Sect. Much of their teaching was faultless, and it has been given to them to stir up thousands of their countrymen to a purer life, and a truer conception of the Almighty. But a mere system of morality can never hold together a great sect. The religious element in the revival soon began to lose its power. Even under the early leaders of the movement it showed signs of wearing out, and the Khalífs had to appeal more and more exclusively to their hearers' detestation of the Infidel.

The Patna Propaganda clearly perceived this, and suited their teachings to the new requirements of the times. Instead of trusting to the terrors of an awakened conscience, they enlisted the more certain and more permanent hatred which the Indian Muhammadans feel towards the English. They thus transferred the basis of their teaching from the noblest capabilities of the Musalmán heart to the fanatical fury of the populace. As time went on, they found it necessary constantly to strengthen the seditious element in their preaching. They converted the Patna Propaganda into a Caravanserai for rebels and traitors. They surrounded it with a labyrinth of walls and outhouses, with one enclosure leading into another by side-doors, and little secret courts in out-of-the-way corners. The early Khalífs had threatened to resist the Magistrate's warrant by force of arms, but their successors found a less dangerous defence in a network of passages, chambers, and outlets. When the Government at length took proceedings against this nest of conspirators, it found it necessary to procure a plan of the buildings, just as if it were dealing with a fortified town. The district missionaries sent up fanatical crowds to the Propaganda. Of these, the greater part, after having their zeal still further stimulated by the lectures of the Patna Leaders, were sent off by detachments to the Camp on the Frontier. The more promising youths were singled out for a longer course of instruction; and after being thoroughly trained in the doctrine of sedition, were returned as colporteurs or missionaries to their own Province.

I have been anxious to do full justice to whatever is good in the history of the Patna Khalífs. Starting with an admirable system of morality, they by degrees abandoned the spiritual element in their teaching, and strengthened their declining cause by appealing to the worst passions of the human heart. I shall afterwards give a sample of the sermons of the Missionaries whom they have trained. Here is a specimen of the teaching by which that training is effected. The Propaganda ceaselessly insists that the Indian Muhammadan who would save himself from hell, has the single alternative of War against the Infidel or Flight[1] from the accursed land. No True Believer can live loyal to our Government without perdition to his soul. 'Those who would deter others from Holy War or Flight are in heart hypocrites. Let all know this. In a country where the ruling religion is other than Muhammadanism, the religious precepts of Muhammad cannot be enforced. It is incumbent on Musalmáns to join together, and wage war upon the Infidels. Those who are unable to take part in the fight should emigrate to a country of the True Faith. At the present time in India, flight is a stern duty. He who denies this, let him declare himself a slave to sensuality. He who, having gone away, returns again, let him know that all his past services are vain. Should he die in India, he will lose the way of salvation.

'In short, Oh Brethren, we ought to weep over our state, for the Messenger of God is angered with us because of our living in the land of the Infidel. When the Prophet of God himself is displeased with us, to whom shall we look for shelter? Those whom God has supplied with the means should resolve upon flight, for a fire is raging here. If we speak the truth, we shall be

[1] *Jihád* or *Hijra.*

hanged; and if we remain silent, injury is done to our faith.'[1]

Besides their seditious literature, and the Central Propaganda at Patna, the Wahábis have a permanent machinery throughout the rural districts for spreading their faith. Dangerous firebrands as the local missionaries sometimes prove, I find it impossible to speak of them without respect. Most of them start life as youths of enthusiastic piety; many of them retain their zeal for religion to the end, with singularly little tincture of the poisonous doctrines in which the Patna preachers have trained them. The civilised man, cribbed within cities, and only permitted to move about this world clogged with luggage, and in the ceaseless society of fellow-travellers, can with difficulty realise the unencumbered life and isolated wanderings of the Wahábi Missionary. We all feel that the soul gathers sanctity in solitude, and perhaps the pilgrim on his lonely foot journey through forest and over mountain thinks purer and fresher thoughts than the work-a-day in-door world. Certain it is that the Wahábi Missionary furnishes, so far as my experience goes, the most spiritual and least selfish type of the sect. Englishmen love to believe that their ancestors, when at their best, lived more in the open in Merry England than we do now; and childhood leaves no more refreshing memories to the life-wearied man than reminiscences of the out-door scenery through which, in the great Christian allegory, the pilgrim passes from the town of Destruction to the Celestial City.

This Forest of Arden spirit reached its highest development in ancient India, where the friendliness of

[1] Jama Tafásír, printed at Dehli, 1867. *Calcutta Review*, cii. p. 391. The first paragraph is condensed from *idem*, p. 393.

nature rendered unnecessary those contrivances which in colder climates elevate man's shelter into his home. The Sanskrit scheme of life required that each householder sprung from the chosen race should, after begetting children into the world, leave his kindred and dwell apart in the forest. Every popular tale introduces us to some venerable eremite beside a running stream, and the most charming scenes of Sakuntalá are those which discover the maiden surrounded by tame fawns in her forest glade. The Wahábi leaders have skilfully availed themselves of this national hankering in India after a solitary life. Even the refuse of great cities, when they have exhausted their fortunes by dissipation, or wearied out by their crimes the patience of the law, can obtain a sort of sanctity by joining a religious order, and retiring to the mountains, or travelling companionless from province to province. Much more does the blameless, lonely life of the Wahábi Missionary render him an object of interest to the villagers upon his route. Throughout many months of the year he enters the door of no human dwelling. He comes from a distant Province, and during the long journey he admits no companion, save perhaps a faithful disciple, to interrupt his self-communings. His serenity of demeanour and indifference to external surroundings make him a visibly different being from ordinary men. It is not surprising, therefore, that the villagers cluster around him, and forget for a moment their disputes about water-courses, and their long standing boundary feuds. The preacher does not always inculcate treason, but only those doctrines which lead their adopters into treason; doctrines which, to use Bacon's impressive aphorism, do dissolve and deface the laws of charity and of human society, and bring down the spirit of God, instead of in the likeness of a dove, in the shape of a vulture or raven. Some of the missionaries, indeed, refrain altogether from poisonous teachings of this sort. In 1870, when travelling through the fanatical Eastern Districts of Bengal, I heard of such a case; and I should be very sorry if I were supposed to use the term Wahábi as a synonym for traitor. A Wahábi preacher had appeared in a lonely village, and forthwith several thousand Muhammadans gathered around him. The Hindus of the neighbourhood dreaded one of those outbursts of zeal against the Infidel in which such conventicles often end, and hurried off messengers to the Headquarters of the District for help. But the preacher, while fulminating against the corrupt life and idolatrous practices of his Muhammadan hearers, refused altogether to touch upon the doctrine of Religious Rebellion. Such mere moralities were by no means what the people had come out into the wilderness to hear, and the disappointed multitude melted away. By the time the Hindu messengers returned, they found the so-called apostle of treason absolutely deserted by his co-religionists, and dependent upon the Hindu villagers for fire and a little rice.

Generally speaking, the Wahábi Missionary has little to fear from the British Officers of the Districts through which he passes; and, indeed, his favourite preaching-ground is the open shady space thronged with suitors outside the Magistrate's Court. The first preacher whose acquaintance I made was encamped in the avenue of the Commissioner's Circuit House. It was only an old man talking to a group of Musalmáns under a *pipal* tree. Close by, an undersized reddish pony, with a large head fixed on a lanky neck, tried to switch off the flies from a saddle-gall by means of a very ragged tail. The poor beast, his fore-feet tied together with grass rope, hopped painfully from one tuft of verdure to another, occasionally turning his head round savagely on some fly beyond the reach of the ragged tail, but soon relapsing with outstretched neck into the listlessness of an animal utterly worn out with travel. The old man had a fresh complexion and a long white beard. He mumbled his words a little, but not enough to hide the vigorous North-country inflection with which he delivered his sentences. He himself seemed very much in earnest, but his eight or ten hearers listened with stupid eyes, and, saving a slight obeisance when they departed, came and went with all the freedom of a street preacher's congregation in England. It was the month of May, and the old man vehemently denounced the follies of the coming festival. By no means careful not to offend, he told his hearers that they would wear their new clothes on their old hearts; that they would stun their ears with the lutes and drums of the Bengáli unbelievers till they were deaf to the simple truths of the Kurán; and that the whole festival of the Muharram, its sham fights, its feigned mourning, its wild feasting, its mock penitence, were utterly abominable to God and his Prophet.

The Musalmáns of a quiet village in Western Bengal are not the best sort of soil for a Reformer to cast his seed into; and as the group broke up at the close of the harangue, public opinion, although divided, was mainly against the preacher. One said: 'This man would have us let the lamp go out at the tomb of our father.' Another: 'He forbids the drums and dancing-girls at the marriage of our daughters.' A third was more favourable: 'Yet he knows the seventy-seven thousand six hundred and thirty-nine words of the Kurán. He says well too, that the Book (Al-Kitáb) bids us pray only to God. Truly he is a Doctor of the Law.' This view, however, was controverted by a Mulla, or crier from the Mosque, who authoritatively ended the discussion. 'This fellow,' he said, 'is a follower of the false Imám who took the Holy Cities by the sword, closed up the path of pilgrimage, and wrote on the door of the Pure House, "There is no God but one God, and Sa'úd is his Prophet"' (Lá iláha illa-lláh, Sa'úd Rasúl illáh).

Altogether the sermon fell rather flat, and the preacher was aware of it. The crowd, when dispersed, left a residue of two Musalmáns in very soiled clothes, who appeared to be fellow-travellers of the preacher, and who watched his every motion with reverence. He talked to them in low earnest tones for some time, and then composed himself to sleep, while his dirty disciples fanned him by turns. The jaded pony, too, gave up any further search after the parched tufts of grass, and, forgetful of his daily wrongs, went to sleep standing under an adjacent tree. In the cool of the evening the party departed as it came, unnoticed; the old man on the little pony, and the two soiled followers trudging along on either side of him.

It must be remembered that the Indian Wahábis are only a small fragment of a great sect. The unsuccessful preacher is the representative of many thousand earnest men at this moment wandering over Asia, sometimes acknowledged, sometimes ignored, at the mosques; speaking various tongues, but all devoted to the one great work of purifying the creed of Muhammad, as Hildebrand's monks purged the Church of Rome.

It is one of the misfortunes attendant on the British Rule in India, that this Reformation should be inseparably linked with hatred against the Infidel Conquerors.

But everywhere, any attempt by the Muhammadans to return to the first principles of their Faith involves a revolt against the ruling power; for even the most orthodox Musalmán State has had to mould those principles to the necessities of Civil Government. Mecca itself, the stronghold of Islám, is the place throughout all the world where the sect is most feared and detested. In the last few pages I have sketched the Wahábi emissary under his milder aspects; but many of them are simply men who live by pandering to the fanatical sedition of the lowest classes of their countrymen. The following is a specimen of the harangues by which they perpetuate the old Muhammadan hatred against British Rule. The first duty of a Musalmán is Religious Rebellion; and to those who reply that such Rebellion is impracticable under the British Power, they answer that the only alternative is flight. The land, and everything that grows on it, are accursed so long as an Infidel Government rules. I have already given examples of the Wahábi exhortations to Holy War, in prose and verse. Here are the arguments by which they persuade the ignorant peasantry of Eastern Bengal, that as they cannot rise *en masse*, the only way to escape eternal torment is to quit their homesteads, and emigrate wholesale from the country of the Infidel:—

'In the name of God. The merciful and kind God is all goodness. He is the Lord of the Universe. May divine kindness and safety attend Muhammad — His Messenger — and all his descendants and companions. Know ye that all Muhammadans are bound to leave a country which is governed by the Infidel, in which acting according to the Muhammadan law is forbidden by the ruling power. If they do not abandon it, then in the hour of death, when their souls will be separated from their bodies, they will suffer great torments. When the Angel of Death will come to separate their souls from their bodies, he will ask them this question: Was not the kingdom of God spacious enough to enable you to leave your homes and settle in another country? And saying this, he will subject them to great pain in separating their souls from their bodies. Afterwards they will suffer the torments of the grave without intermission, and on the Day of Judgment they will be cast into hell, where they will suffer eternal punishment. May God forbid that Muhammadans should die in a country ruled over by the Infidel.

'Make your escape now. Go to a country which is governed by Musalmáns, and live there in the land of the Faithful. If you reach it alive, then all the sins of your life will be forgiven. Do not trouble yourself about the means of livelihood. God, who provides for all, will give you food wherever you may be.

'In the Holy Traditions it is written how an Israelite who had murdered ninety-nine men went to a man of God, confessed his crimes, and asked how he could obtain forgiveness. The man of God answered: "If any person unjustly kills even one man, he will certainly be damned. Your sins will not be forgiven; you will certainly go to hell." Hearing this, the Israelite said: "I must go to hell, that is certain. I shall therefore kill you in order to make up a hundred murders." He then killed the holy man, and, going to another holy man, confessed that he had committed one hundred murders, and asked how he could obtain forgiveness. This man of God answered: "By sincere repentance and the performance of Flight from the land of the Infidel." As soon as he heard this he repented of his sins, and leaving his country, set out for a foreign land. On the way death approached, and both the Angels—viz. the Angel of Mercy and the Angel of Punishment—appeared to separate his soul from his body. The Angel of Mercy said that he would separate the man's soul from his body because he had repented of his sins and performed Flight. The Angel of Punishment admitted that if the man had succeeded in reaching another kingdom, the office would have belonged to the Angel of Mercy; but that he claimed the right of performing the operation, and of subjecting the man to torments, because he had not succeeded in completing the Flight to a land of the True Believers. Then both Angels measured the land on which the man was lying, and found that one of his feet had crossed the boundary, and lay within a kingdom of Islám. On this the Angel of Mercy, declaring that his right was established, painlessly separated the soul from his body, and the man was admitted amongst the favoured of God. You have heard how Religious Flight is rewarded in the next world. Therefore pray to God for grace to enable all of you to perform Flight, and to perform it quickly, lest you die in an infidel country.'[1]

But besides their teeming literature of treason, their Central Propaganda at Patna, and their Missionaries wandering throughout the length and breadth of Bengal, the Wahábis have invented a fourth organisation for reaching the seditious masses. The earlier Khalífs favoured the efforts of their emissaries to effect a permanent settlement wherever the multitude of their converts encouraged their doing so. A number of Traitor Settlements have thus been established throughout rural Bengal. These District-Centres of treason keep up a

[1] Abbreviated from *Calcutta Review*, cii. pp. 388–389.

regular correspondence with the Propaganda at Patna, and each has its own machinery for raising money and recruits, complete within itself. In 1870 two such District-Centres were broken up, and their chief preachers, after impartial trial by the Courts, sentenced to transportation for life and forfeiture of property. The evidence which then came out might well appal any alien Government less confident in its own integrity than that of British India. I shall briefly narrate the history of one of the prisoners.

About thirty years ago, one of the Khalífs[1] came on a missionary tour to Maldah District in Lower Bengal. The field proving good, he settled for several years in a village, married one of the daughters of the place, and established himself as a schoolmaster. The children of the petty proprietors flocked to the learned man, and in this way he insinuated himself into the landed families of the District. He preached rebellion with great force and unction, accustomed the people to a regular system of contributions for the Holy War, and forwarded yearly supplies of money and men to the Propaganda at Patna, for transmission to the Frontier Camp. One of his tax-collectors,[2] whom he had raised from the rank of an ordinary peasant, turned out to be a man of zeal and talent. He received a fourth of the collections as salary, and gradually became a ruling elder in the village. For many years he carried on his business undisturbed, but about 1853 the Magistrate's suspicions were aroused. The religious tax-gatherer's house was searched, and letters were found proving the seditious character of his trade,

[1] Abd-ur-rahmán, a native of Lucknow, appointed to the Caliphate by one of the original Khalífs, Wiláyat Alí.

[2] Rafík Mandal.

and his connection with the Holy War which the Frontier Camp had shortly before tried to stir up in the Panjáb.[1]

The District-Centre was arrested, but, with our usual contempt for petty conspirators, was shortly afterwards released. His brief imprisonment sufficed, however, to make it dangerous for him to continue his treasonable levies, and he resigned his office as religious tax-gatherer to his son.[2] His successor proved himself worthy of the post; and, to use the neutral-tinted and indeed gently appreciative words of the officer in charge of his case,[3] 'from that time up to the date of his trial, he seems to have honestly exerted himself to the utmost in sustaining the Religious War by recruits.' All this he did wholly undisturbed by the District Authorities. An English Magistrate in India has the reluctance of a prefect of the Augustan Empire to intermeddle with the various beliefs or superstitions of the races over whom he rules. Treason can thus safely walk about under a religious habit. But the State Trial[4] at Patna in 1865 disclosed the Maldah District-Centre's share in the general conspiracy. In spite of this warning, however, he continued his levies of money and men for the Frontier War; openly went from village to village preaching rebellion; and in 1868, when he found the liberality of his people slackening, brought down the son of the Patna Khalíf to assist him in reviving their zeal. His jurisdiction extended over

[1] In 1852, when the 4th Native Infantry were tampered with, and the Patna Magistrate reported the growth of the sect, and their determination to resist further inquiries in that city by force of arms.

[2] Maulaví Amír-ud-dín of Maldah.

[3] Report filed with the Record of the Maldah Trial of 1870. Official Papers.

[4] In the matter of Maulaví Ahmad-ullah, who was convicted of treason, and sentenced by the Sessions Court to death and forfeiture of property, the capital part of his sentence being afterwards mitigated to transportation for life.

three separate Districts;[1] and for several days' journey down the Ganges the ignorant Musalmán peasantry on both banks, and on the islands which the river has thrown up in its bed, owned his control. The number of recruits whom he sent to the Frontier Camp can never be ascertained; but at a single one of the Traitor outposts on our Frontier, containing 430 fighting men, more than ten per cent. had been supplied from his jurisdiction.

His system of pecuniary levies was simple and complete. He grouped together the villages into fiscal clusters, and to each cluster he appointed a chief tax-gatherer. This officer, on his part, appointed a village collector to every hamlet, checked their collections, and transmitted the proceeds to the District-Centre. As a rule, each village had one tax-gatherer; but in populous villages a larger staff was employed, consisting of the priest,[2] who led the prayers and gathered the contributions; the general manager[3] or Deacon, who looked after the worldly affairs of the sect; and an officer[4] who supplied messengers for dangerous letters, and for transmitting the oblations of treason.

These oblations are of four kinds. The first is a tax of two and a half per cent. on all property held in possession during the lunar year. It bears the name of 'Legal Alms,'[5] and has from the first been devoted to war against the Infidel. This tax, however, only falls upon property above a certain value, and the Patna Khalíf[6] on his return from the Frontier Camp found its proceeds inadequate to support the Holy War. He accordingly appropriated the voluntary alms given for indigent persons at the Mosque, and thus confiscated the patri-

[1] Including the whole of Maldah, and parts of the Districts of Murshidabad and Rájsháhí.

[2] Dín-ke-sardár. [3] Dunya-ke-sardár. [4] Dák-ke-sardár.

[5] Zakát. [6] Ináyat Alí.

mony of the poor to the purpose of rapine and revolt. Such alms are bestowed as a solemn religious duty on the great Muhammadan festival of the year. To the month of fasting and humiliation[1] succeeds an ecstasy of religious rejoicing.[2] But before entering the Mosque to hear the festival prayers, the devout Musalmán believes that he must distribute of his substance to the poor, or the whole penance of the past thirty days will be refused by God. It was these offerings[3] which the Patna Khalíf swept into the Traitors' purse. He also invented a new tax, from which even the poorest could not escape. He commanded every head of a family to put aside a handful[4] of rice for each member of his household at every meal, and to deposit it after the Friday prayers with the village collector. In this way stores of grain were gathered together, and publicly sold on behoof of the Holy War. Such imposts, however, represented only the minimum which the religious tax-gatherers had a right to exact. The provident Khalíf took care that ample scope should be given for the zeal of new converts, or for the sudden impulses produced by a stirring sermon. He accordingly devised an extraordinary cess, to be bestowed at intervals as a voluntary donation, over and above the regular taxes which his collectors demanded as a matter of right. The tax-gatherers-in-chief made an annual tour, each through his own group of villages, at the time of the great festival, and took care that every family had paid up its dues for the past twelve months in full.

District-Centres of equal ability in levying money and recruits are scattered over Bengal, and the unfortunate man whom I have selected as an example was only

[1] Ramazán.

[2] 'Id-ul-fitr, or Ramazán-ki-'íd.

[3] Fitr.

[4] Mutthi.

one of many. His Headquarters lay upon the great thoroughfare from Lower Bengal to the North-West, and formed a halting-place for every seditious preacher who travelled up or down. The two Khalífs who testified to the death on the Frontier[1] had partaken of his hospitality. One of the present leaders of the Rebel Camp[2] had also stayed with him *en route;* and many District-Centres, together with the heads of the Patna Propaganda, have been his guests. His town[3] formerly lay on the right bank of the Ganges, at a distance from the Headquarters of the District, or from any police village belonging to it. Even the great convulsions of nature which destroyed the town helped to spread the cause. The Ganges, in one of its huge writhings backwards and forwards across the country, ate away the land on its right bank, so that not a vestige of the Wahábi Settlement remains. The inhabitants dispersed, some to a newly-formed island near the left bank of the river, others to various inland hamlets; and wherever they went, each little party became a centre of sedition. As the river throws up new land, a Wahábi colony immediately takes possession, and forms the nucleus of a new village.

It may well be supposed that so permanent and so widely spread a disaffection has caused grave anxiety to the Indian Government. During the past seven years, one traitor after another has been convicted and transported for life. Indeed, each of the fanatic wars on our Frontier has produced its corresponding State Trial within our Territory. At this moment a large body of prisoners, drawn from widely distant Districts, are suffering for their common crimes or awaiting their trial. Since the first edition of this work appeared, a month ago, another band,

[1] Ináyat Alí and Maksúd Alí. [2] Fyáz Alí. [3] Naráyanpur.

five in number, have been sentenced by the Sessions' Court to transportation for life. It is difficult to speak of those who have been convicted without prejudice to the chance of escape of those who have yet to be tried; for the evidence already on record mixes up the names of both. Yet these State Trials form one of the most curious phenomena in Indian History; and without using the details furnished by them, it is impossible to follow the ramifications of the chronic conspiracy in Bengal. I shall therefore select the one which is furthest removed from the pending proceedings in point of time, and carefully exclude everything which might tend to the prejudice of any of the unfortunate men awaiting their trial, but not yet adjudged guilty by the law.

The trial of 1864 was the natural outcome of the disastrous fanatic war in 1863. Unlike the judicial proceedings of previous years, it was no longer a few sepoys of a Native Regiment, or an isolated preacher of sedition, whose treason had to be inquired into, but a widely ramified conspiracy spread over distant Provinces, and furnished with ample machinery for secrecy and self-defence. In July 1864, Sir Herbert Edwardes, as Sessions Judge at Ambálla, delivered judgment in a State Trial which had occupied the Court during nearly twenty sittings. Eleven Musalmán subjects of the British Crown stood at the bar charged with high treason. Among them were representatives of every rank of Muhammadan society: priests of the highest family, an army contractor and wholesale butcher, a scrivener, a soldier, an itinerant preacher, a house-steward, and a husbandman. They had been defended by English Counsel; they had had the full advantage both of technical pleas in bar and of able pleadings on the merits of the case; six of their countrymen had sat as Assessors with the Judge on the bench; and the trial ended in the condemnation of eight of them to transportation for life, and of the remaining three to the last penalty of the law.

The vast Northern Presidency contains races of many shades of colour, and of great diversity of dialect; and it would be easier for an Italian to pass as an Englishman in London, than for a Bengáli to play the Panjábi at Pesháwar. Our officers noticed, during the frontier campaign of 1858, that numbers of the enemy slain in battle had the unmistakeable dark, sallow complexion which is imparted by the steamy swamps of Lower Bengal. The clue, however, could not be followed up at that time. At the end of the campaign the Irregular Horse were reduced, and several of the deserving men enrolled in the Mounted Police. One of them, a Panjábi Musalmán,[1] soon rose to the rank of sergeant in a District[2] near Ambálla. In May 1863, while on his rounds one morning, he descried four foreigners proceeding along the Great North Road. Their diminutive stature, dingy complexion, and puny beards, reminded the old soldier of the Bengáli traitors he had seen amid the dead on the battle-field in 1858. He got into conversation with them, worked himself into their secrets, and at length elicited that they were Bengáli emissaries from Malká, on their way back to their native province to arrange for the forwarding of fresh supplies of money and men.

The tall Northerner at once arrested the four traitors. They appealed to him as a brother Muhammadan, and offered him any bribe he would name, to be paid by a certain scrivener, Ja'far Khán, in the neighbouring market town of Tháneswar. But the old soldier proved faithful to

[1] Guzan Khán by name. [2] Karnál.

his salt, and forthwith sent them before the Magistrate. There can be little doubt, if that officer had at once committed these four Bengális, the whole conspiracy would have been detected; the Fanatics would not have ventured to attack our Guide Corps; and the British Empire would have been spared a bloody campaign. But at that time the Empire was in profound peace; Tháneswar is a quiet inland district; High Treason is a rare crime; false charges by the Indian Police for the purpose of extorting money are the commonest occurrences. The Magistrate, in refusing to commit the four peaceable wayfarers, only acted in the way which, in ninety-nine out of a hundred cases, would have been consonant with substantial justice.

This, however, happened to be the hundredth case.

The Sergeant of Mounted Police took affront at the release of his prisoners. The feeling that his report had been doubted preyed upon his high Panjábi spirit, and he still felt perfectly certain that a great unseen danger was about to break upon our Empire.

He devised an enterprise hardly surpassed in the legends of Spartan fortitude or the annals of Roman fidelity. To abandon his post without leave would have been desertion; but he had a son in his native village, far in the North, whom he loved better than anything upon earth, except the family honour. Between his village and the Frontier lay our outposts, all on the alert to stop any stray plunderer or absconding traitor. Beyond the Frontier were the Fanatics, on the eve of their great act of overt hostility to the Crown, and in the last degree suspicious of any stranger not forwarded in the regular manner by their agents within our Empire. The father, well knowing that his son, if he escaped being hanged at our outposts as a traitor on his way to join the Rebel Camp, ran a very imminent risk of being strangled by the Wahábis as a spy, commanded his boy in the name of the family honour to go to Malká, and not to return till he could bring back the names of the conspirators within our territory who were aiding the Fanatics outside.

The son received the letter, and next day disappeared from the village. What were his sufferings and hair-breadth escapes, none but his own family knows. But it came out in evidence that he completely deceived the Wahábis, joined in their descent upon Sittána, repassed our outposts unscathed, and turning neither to the left nor to the right, presented himself one evening at his father's hut, many hundred miles inland, worn out by travel, want, and disease, but charged with the secret, 'that Munshi Ja'far of Tháneswar, whom men call Khalífa, was the great man who passed up the Bengális and their carbines and rifles.' Now Ja'far was the scrivener in the market town of Tháneswar, who would have at once paid the bribe, if the Sergeant had let the four travellers go.

I can recall no more touching picture of *prisca fides* than that stern Panjábi father, riding proudly and silently on his daily rounds, brooding over his distrusted word, and, as the months passed, growing sick and more sick regarding the fate of the son, whose life he had imperilled to redeem his honour, and to save the foreign masters who had doubted it. Before such a revenge our cautious English sense of duty must stand penitent and uncovered. Yet it is some comfort to remember that, if the Indian Government has at times committed grave mistakes, it has not forgotten amply to redress them.

The private history of Ja'far, scrivener in the market town of Tháneswar, is full of interest. Born in a very humble rank, he raised himself by force of character to Headman[1] of his township. One day he chanced to stop and listen to the discourse of an itinerant Wahábi preacher. The religious feelings of the prosperous townsman were awakened. He pondered upon the corrupted ceremonial of the mosques, and after passing through a deep spiritual darkness, not unlike that which John Bunyan experienced, he openly professed himself a Wahábi, and threw his whole nature into the work of religious reform.

The new convert devoted much time to self-examination, and rigidly kept account with his soul. He began to write his religious experiences; and these, under the title of the Counsels of Ja'far, form one of the most interesting documents ever filed in a State Trial.

'I commence writing this book on Tuesday, 18th Zulhijja, 1278 Hijra.[2] The completion is in the hand of God. I have not followed any particular method, but simply note down the events, both relating to the Faith and to the world, in which I have from time to time taken part. I further wish to make known that this world is transitory. Man, genie, angel, beast, tree, whatsoever has had its origin in it, shall perish each at its appointed time. None but God remains eternal. Whoever has come into the world, had he lived for 1000 years, has carried nothing away with him but remorse. My own state is as follows. Up to ten years of age I received no education. On my father's death, when I was about ten or twelve, and my younger brother only six months, I came under the guardianship of my mother, who was quite uneducated, and whose religious training had been

[1] Lambardár, or Fiscal Representative of the township, in dealing with the officers of Government.

[2] June 1862.

neglected. As a boy I took no thought of learning, and used to wander about as a vagabond; but when I got a little sense, I commenced reading.

'Associating myself with the Petition-writers in 1856, it came to pass that all the Pleaders and Petition-writers consulted me as to the Rules, Regulations, and Acts of the Legislature, and I came to be above them all.' Petition-writers were a sort of unregistered pettifoggers, who wrote out the plaints of suitors in the Magistrate's Court, at a fee varying from sixpence to two shillings. Ja'far had a large practice, but the money thus gained in the Infidel's Court seemed to do him no good; 'on the contrary, by this profession I obtained great injury to my faith. It is not well to follow this calling. Had I not adopted it, my religious state would have been much better. My mode of livelihood has been detrimental to me in regard to the pleasures of worshipping and of high piety. When I had leisure from the Courts, even for a couple of days, my state became good. The mere contact with the Musalmán *employés* of the Unbeliever, which was the drawback attending my position, acted as poison on my soul.'

Ja'far's legal reputation spread notwithstanding his dislike of the profession, and he was retained as family adviser by some of the powerful landholders in the neighbourhood. He seems to have been a singularly sincere man, never allowing his temporal success to interfere with his eternal interests. Every one who came near him owned his influence, and, like Muhammad, he began by converting his own household. One of these, his clerk, remained faithful to his master in his direst extremity, and stood by his side as a fellow-witness to the Faith in the dock of the Sessions Court at Ambálla.

When the mutiny of 1857 broke out, Ja'far chose

twelve of his most trustworthy disciples, and repaired to the Rebel Camp. Even in the unwonted work of fighting his force of character made him conspicuous, and he gained the reputation of being a man fit to be trusted with treasonable secrets. Upon the downfall of the rebel hopes at Dehli, he returned to his attorney's business at Thánes-war, brooding over the inscrutable decree of Providence which had given victory to the Unbelievers, and more than ever discontented with what he calls 'this exceedingly dirty business of Petition-writing.' Open force had failed, and it remained to be seen what could be effected by secret conspiracy. Ja'far soon became a member of the widespread Wahábi confederacy. His secret duties threw a religious halo even over his detested profession; for 'be it known,' he writes at this period, 'I do this by order of a Certain Person, and for a Hidden Object.'[1]

This Certain Person was Maulaví Yahya Alí of Patna, Spiritual Director of the Wahábi sect in India. The Hidden Object was the forwarding of recruits and munitions of war to the Wahábi colony on the Mahában, then in open hostilities against the British Crown.

I have already described the Patna Propaganda, of which Yahya Alí was then the head. Long before the trial of 1864 the place had been known throughout India as a hospice of the reformed sect. The buildings lay on the left hand side of the Sadikpur Lane, with a considerable frontage, and ran back some distance from the street. Their exteriors had that mournful dilapidated look which the brick and stucco buildings of India assume after the first

[1] Sir Herbert Edwardes, in delivering sentence, thus summed up Ja'far's character:—'It is impossible to exceed the bitter hostility, treasonable activity, and mischievous ability of this prisoner. He is an educated man, and a Headman in his village. There is no doubt of his guilt, and no palliation of it.'—Record of the Ambálla State Trial in 1864; Official Papers.

wet season, and which presents such a squalid contrast to our preconceptions of the gorgeous East. The most important edifice of the group was a very plain mosque, in which public prayer was offered up each hour of the day, and a khotba or sermon every Friday. These Friday lectures were vehement harangues, insisting above all on the duty of War against the Infidel, but also exposing the inefficacy of works without faith, warning the hearers of their great spiritual danger, and urging them to cultivate the Inward Life. They contrasted the simple worship of the Prophet with the cumbrous ritual, the endless mummeries, bowings, and genuflexions of the mosques, and bitterly inveighed against those who refused to accept the Wahábi alternative of Insurrection or Flight.

Generally speaking, they inculcated a spiritual standard much higher than ordinary natures are capable of; and the hearers, although deeply impressed at the moment, carried away only a permanent recollection of having been rendered exceedingly uncomfortable. The preachers of some of the other city mosques, moreover, while forced to acknowledge the learning and eloquence of the Sadikpur Lane preachers, denounced them as rejecters of holy sacraments and unitarian schismatics.

Yahya Alí, Chief Priest and Khalíf, ruled over the Propaganda with a firm but gentle hand. The recruits whom the itinerant missionaries sent up in flocks from the Districts of Lower Bengal he kindly received at the hospice. The better sort of them he carefully trained up as preachers, while those destined immediately for the Rebel Camp were handed over to a lay brother, who fanned their zeal for the conflict without troubling them very much with matters of doctrine. This lay brother[1] was the bursar of

[1] Abd-ul-ghaffár.

the Propaganda, and a most useful man. Not less expert than Chaucer's 'gentil manciple,' he managed the whole temporal affairs of the hospice, daily harangued the recruits on the high duty of Holy War, and even delivered occasional prelections on divinity to the theological students, when the Chief Priest, under whose care they properly fell, was otherwise engaged. What he did, he did with perfect sincerity of heart, and at the last stood undaunted by his master's side in the dock at Ambálla.

The Chief Priest, Yahya Alí, had many duties. He corresponded with all the itinerant preachers as Spiritual Director of the sect in India. He organised and personally worked a complicated system of drafts in a secret language, by which he safely transmitted large sums from the centre of the Empire to the Rebel Camp beyond the Frontier. He conducted the public ministrations in the mosque. He examined and passed the rifles for the Fanatic Host, delivered a course of divinity lectures to the students, and by private study acquired an intimate acquaintance with the Arabic Fathers.

But the most delicate operation of the conspirators was the transmission of recruits from the Patna Propaganda, or Little Warehouse, as it was called in their secret language, to the Great Warehouse or Rebel Camp beyond the Frontier. The Bengáli convert was liable to a hundred awkward questions *en route.* He had to march nearly two thousand miles across the wide provinces of the North-West and the Panjáb, where in every village his physical appearance and language stamped him as a foreigner. It was in this dangerous work that Yahya Alí's genius for administration most fully developed itself. He organised a system of Wahábi hospices along the route, and placed each under the charge of a proven disciple. He thus divided the Great North Road into convenient sections, and the traitors on their way to the Rebel Camp journeyed in safety through strange Provinces, in the full assurance that at the end of each stage there were friends upon the look-out for their arrival. The heads of the wayside hospices were men of diverse ranks of life, but all devoted to the overthrow of the British Rule, and each the president of a local committee of conspirators. Yahya Alí showed an admirable knowledge of character in selecting these men, for neither fear of detection nor hope of reward induced a single one of them to appear against their leader in the hour of his fall.

Above all, he was a man of good birth, and kept things smooth with the British authorities at Patna. One of his family held an honorary post under our Government, while another led the Fanatic Host in its raids upon our Frontier. Seldom have more impressive words been uttered in a Court of Justice than those in which Sir Herbert Edwardes passed sentence of death upon this man:—

'It is proved,' he said, 'against the prisoner Yahya Alí, that he has been the mainspring of the great treason which this trial has laid bare. He has been the religious preacher, spreading from his mosque at Patna, under the most solemn sanctions, the hateful principles of the Crescentade. He has enlisted subordinate Agents to collect money and preach the Moslem Jihád (War against the Infidel). He has deluded hundreds and thousands of his countrymen into treason and rebellion. He has plunged the Government of British India, by his intrigues, into a Frontier War, which has cost hundreds of lives. He is a highly educated man, who can plead no excuse of ignorance. What he has done, he has done with forethought, resolution, and the bitterest treason. He belongs to a hereditarily disloyal and fanatical family. He aspires to the merit of a religious reformer; but instead of appealing to reason and to conscience, like his Hindu fellow-countrymen in Bengal, of the Bráhma Samáj, he seeks his end in political revolution, and madly plots against the Government, which probably saved the Muhammadans of India from extinction, and certainly brought in religious freedom.'

Ja'far the Scrivener, and Yahya Alí the Chief Priest, have claimed the first place among the prisoners of 1864, as the two religious heads of the Conspiracy. But even their talents for treason pale before those of Muhammad Sháfi', wholesale butcher in Dehli, and meat supplier to the British Forces in the Panjáb. This man was the son of one of the great trading houses of Northern India. The origin of his family's connection with Government takes us back to the wars of Warren Hastings and Lord Cornwallis. Muhammad's great-grandfather and grandfather were humble graziers, who, partly by speculation, partly by rigid economy, raised themselves considerably in the world. It was a period better fitted for making fortunes than for keeping them. War prices ruled, and the armies, constantly in motion, compelled our Commissariat to seek the acquaintance of the cattle-contractors of Northern India. It is possible that the family fortunes of the traitor owed their rise to the great famine of 1769, which first awakened the people of England to their responsibilities in India. During the last decades of the century, I find the grandfather in a highly responsible position, executing heavy contracts to the perfect satisfaction of the officers in charge of the Commissariat. Muhammad's father greatly enlarged the scope of these transactions. Besides the money required for advances to the smaller cattle-breeders, he had a surplus capital which he lent out on the safest securities, and at the highest interest. His son succeeded to a vast fortune, but true to the Indian instinct of following his father's craft, he devoted himself with energy to the family trades; and it was as a great banker and wholesale butcher that he carried on the nefarious operations which landed him in the condemned cell at Ambálla.

As the Chief Priest was the head, so this man was the right hand of the Conspiracy.

He had agencies in all the chief cities of Hindustán, and held the meat contracts for the seven chief British Cantonments along the Great North Road. Connected by blood or by commercial ties with the richest trading houses of the Panjáb, he formed the centre of an ever-widening circle of dependants, spread all over Upper India; and his business brought him into contact with the shepherd tribes far beyond our frontier. He yearly received many hundred thousand pounds from the British Government; in his dealings he was punctual, and obedient to servility; and he so hoodwinked the Commissariat Officers, that he obtained a renewal of his meat contracts for the troops, even after he had been charged with treason to the Queen.

The widespread influence which he thus acquired as our servant, he applied to our destruction. He was the banker of the Conspiracy, and skilfully used the conveniences for transferring money, which Government granted to him as an Army Contractor, to aid and succour the Rebel Camp. He had nothing of the religious enthusiast about him. He allowed no foolish fanaticism to lead him into any indiscretion. He was guilty of no saintly self-sacrifice. He appears throughout the keen, sharp-sighted, sordid schemer, deliberately entering into the most perilous transactions for a correspondingly high profit, and trusting to his clear intellect and high position to guide him safe through the dangers which beset his path.

Ja'far the Scrivener, and Yahya Alí the Priest, made no pretensions to loyalty, and sought nothing at our hands. Earnest, conscientious men, they pricked themselves with the poisoned weapons which a false religion had put into their hands; and now that, Laertes-like, they have paid the price of their treachery, history may dwell with emotions almost akin to pity on their fate. But for Muhammad Sháfi' there can be no such feeling. He licked our hand in order to bite it. He took usury from his fellow-conspirators, and conducted with a safe margin of profit an underwriting business in treasonable risks. He stands out from the band of religionists and minor traitors whom the State Trial of 1864 brought together in the Ambálla dock, as one of those gigantic villains whom the downfall of the Roman Republic produced, and whom the orations of Cicero have handed down. He combined the heartlessness of Oppianicus with the caution of Lentulus; and his one fatal step was in not deserting the pirates before the man-of-war hove in sight.

I have now sketched the four chief figures[1] in the group of traitors who, day after day, stood together in the Ambálla Court. I shall briefly dismiss the other

[1] Yahya Alí, the Chief Priest; Abd-ul-ghaffár, the bursar of the Propaganda at Patna; Ja'far, the scrivener of Tháneswar, who forwarded the recruits through the Panjáb; and Muhammad Sháfi', the meat supplier to the British Forces, who cashed the treasonable remittances, and used his position as an Army Contractor to give information as to the movements of our troops.

eight with the words in which the Judge passed sentence upon them :—

'It is proved against the prisoner Rahim, that at his house these treasons have been carried on. In his premises the Bengáli Crescentaders gathered and were lodged. It was his servant who kept the treasure, fed the recruits, and remitted the subscriptions to the Fanatics; and it was his brother-in-law, Yahya Alí, who preached treason at the door of his *zenana*. His ability is inferior to Yahya Alí's, and he is not so conspicuous; but he has done what in him lay against the State.

'It is proved against Ilahi Baksh, that he has been the channel through which the Patna Maulavis forwarded the funds they collected up-country to Ja'far at Thánes-war, to be passed on to Malká and Sittána.

'It is proved against Husaini of Patna, that he is a servant of Ilahi Baksh; that he has been employed by him in effecting remittances for treasonable purposes; that a large sum of gold muhars was received by him from Abd-ul-Ghaffár, under order from Yahya Alí; that he sewed them up in a jacket, and so brought them up-country from Patna to Dehli, where he delivered them, as he had been ordered, to the prisoner Ja'far. It is also proved that he carried up money orders for Rs. 6000, and that he thoroughly understood the treasonable nature of the service on which he was engaged.

'It is proved against Kázi Miyán Ján, that he preached and recruited for the Crescentade in Bengal, and that he has been an active agent for the Patna conspirators and the fanatics in the hills, collecting and remitting funds, forwarding letters, etc. The most treasonable correspondence has been found in his house, from both Patna and Malká, showing also that he had three or four *aliases*.

'It is proved against Abd-ul-Karím that he was the confidential agent of Muhammad Sháfi' (the meat supplier) in cashing the Patna money orders for treasonable purposes, and that he was in communication with Yahya Alí concerning these purposes.

'It is proved against the prisoner Husaini of Thánes-war that he was a confidential agent and go-between of the prisoners Muhammad Ja'far and Muhammad Sháfi' in these treasons, and that he was seized in the act of conveying 290 pieces of gold[1] from Ja'far to Muhammad Sháfi' for remittance to the Queen's enemies.

'It is proved against Abd-ul-Ghaffár, No. 2,[2] that he was a disciple of Yahya Alí at Patna; that Yahya Alí deputed him to be the assistant of the prisoner Ja'far in the rebel recruiting depot at Tháneswar; that he did so assist, and that he corresponded with the prisoner Yahya Alí on treasonable matters.'[3]

The three most conspicuous features of the conspiracy which the trial disclosed, were the admirable sagacity with which so widely spread a treason had been organised; the secrecy with which its complicated operations were conducted; and the absolute fidelity to one another which its members maintained. Its success depended to some extent upon an ingenious system of *aliases*, and upon the secret language of which I give a specimen below.[4] But it is impossible to resist the conviction that the

[1] Gold Muhars.

[2] This was another man of the same name as the Abd-ul-Ghaffár already mentioned.

[3] In this account of the Trial of 1864, I have in some places used an article which I put forth at the time, 1864. All the statements are based upon the Certified Record of the Case, upon Letters from the Local Authorities, or upon *Official Reports*.

[4] A battle is called a lawsuit; God, the Law Agent; Gold Muhars are called large red rubies, large Dehli gold-embroidered shoes, or large red birds;

conspirators, with the exception of the army contractor, were actuated by a conscientious zeal for what they believed to be the cause of God, and by a firm resolve to abide stedfast to the death. The British authorities took the wise revenge of denying even to the most treasonable of them the glory of martyrdom. The highest Court of the Province, after a patient hearing in appeal, confirmed Sir Herbert Edwardes' finding as to their guilt, but modified the capital sentence even in the three most flagrant cases to transportation for life.[1]

The State Trial of 1864 proved as little effective as the retributive campaign of 1863 to check the zeal of the traitors. Their internal dissensions kept them quiet for a few years on the Frontier, but meanwhile they vigorously preached the Holy War within our territory. In Eastern Bengal, every District was tainted with the treason; and the Muhammadan peasantry down the whole course of the Ganges, from Patna to the sea, laid apart weekly offerings in aid of the Rebel Camp. What proportion of these oblations actually reached the Frontier is doubtful; and as the difficulties of transmission increased, the preachers seem to have felt justified in helping themselves more liberally than their earlier zeal would have permitted. The fanatical Musalmáns of the Delta bear the name not of Wahábis, but of Faráizís,[2] or rejecters of all glosses and non-essential parts of Islám. They call themselves the

remittances in Gold Muhars are spoken of as rosaries of red beads, and remittances in money as the price of books and merchandise; drafts or money orders are called white stones, the amount being intimated by the number of white beads as on a rosary.—*Official Papers.*

[1] Paras. 182–184 of the Judgment in Appeal by the Judicial Commissioner of the Panjáb, dated 24th August 1864.

[2] Faráizís (from the Arabic *Farízah*, plural *Faráiz*, the same as *Farz*) are those who admit the obligation of only the first two of the five Muhammadan duties, and reject the other three as not based upon the Kurán or the Hadís. These five sorts of religious commands are: (1st) *Farz* (hence Faráizí), the

New Musalmáns, and muster in vast numbers in the Districts east of Calcutta. We have already seen how, in 1831, a merely local leader got together between three and four thousand men, beat back a detachment of the Calcutta Militia, and was only put down by regular troops. In 1843 the sect had attained such dangerous proportions as to form a subject of special inquiry by Government. The head of the Bengal Police reported that a single one of their preachers had gathered together some eighty thousand followers, who asserted complete equality among themselves, looked upon the cause of each as that of the whole sect, and considered nothing criminal if done in behalf of a brother in distress.[1] The later Khalífs, especially Yahya Alí, amalgamated the Faráizís of Lower Bengal with the Wahábis of Northern India; and during the past thirteen years they have been found side by side alike among the dead on the field of battle, and in the dock of our Courts of Justice.

From 1864 to 1868 the levies of money and men went on as before, and a special establishment had to be organised to deal with the conspiracy. At this moment the cost of watching the Wahábis, and keeping them within bounds, amounts in a single Province to as much as would suffice for the Administration, Judicial and Criminal, of a British District containing one-third of the whole population of Scotland. The evil had so widely

rejection of which makes a man an infidel; (2d) *Wájib*, the rejection of which makes a man a sinful Musalmán; (3d) *Sunnát*, which, if not performed, bring down God's anger or threat (*'itáb*); (4th) *Mustahabb*, the non-fulfilment of which involves no punishment, but which if performed produce religious merit and reward, *e.g.* vows; (5th) *Mubáh*, the performance of which is indifferent. The Faráizís now claim as their founder, not Títu Miyán, but Sharkat-ullah, who preached in Dacca in 1828.

[1] Letters, No. 1001, dated 13th May 1843, and No. 50 of 1847, from the Commissioner of Police for Bengal, etc.

diffused itself, that it was difficult to know where to begin. Each District-Centre spreads disaffection through thousands of families; but the only possible witnesses against him are his own converts, who would prefer death to the betrayal of their master.

In 1868, notwithstanding the exertions of the Police within our territory, and of the military outposts on the Frontier, the fanatic intrigues again involved the Empire in a costly campaign. In the same year the Maldah Head-Centre fearlessly brought down the son of the Patna Khalíf to preach treason in the heart of Bengal. The ordinary action of the Courts proved altogether inadequate to the crisis, and the Government had to have recourse to the special procedure which had been entrusted to it to meet such cases. As far back as 1818, the Legislature formally recognised the perils to which a Government, composed like our own of a small body of foreigners, is perpetually subject from the overwhelming masses of the conquered population. It accordingly vested the Executive with the power of arrest in times of conspiracy. A national peril of this sort would be met in England by a suspension of the Habeas Corpus Act, but such a suspension in India would be a calamity little less terrible than making over the country to Martial Law. In the present instance, for example, it is only a single sect of the Musalmáns who are to blame; and the Musalmán community, although very numerous in Eastern Bengal, forms but one-tenth of the population of India. If any Act corresponding to a general suspension of the Habeas Corpus Act were passed, the Hindus would justly complain that they, the real natives of the country, were made to suffer for the disloyalty of their deadliest enemies, the Muhammadans. Indeed, even among the

Musalmáns themselves, there would be indignant protests by the Sunni and Shiah sects against being placed under a common ban with the Wahábi schismatics.

The injustice would be intensified by an influence, happily unknown in England, but rampant in India. The Bengáli, whether rich or poor, wreaks his malice on a rival, and seeks his revenge against an enemy, not by inconsiderate violence, but by due course of law. He uses the Courts for the same purpose for which an Englishman employs a horse-whip, or a Californian his bowie-knife. A criminal prosecution is the correct form for inflicting personal chastisement, and a general suspension of, in India, what corresponds to the Habeas Corpus Act would place every man at the mercy of his enemies. The Police Returns in India disclose an overwhelming proportion of false complaints to true ones, and the Bengáli has reduced the rather perilous business of making out a *primâ facie* Case to an exact science. A formal interference with the right of Habeas Corpus would give the signal for a paroxysm of perjury. The innocent would live in constant fear of being thrown into prison, and kept there on false charges of treason; the revengeful and malicious would enjoy a perpetual triumph.

Yet, without a power of arrest in time of sedition, similar to that with which the suspension of the Habeas Corpus arms the Queen's Ministers in England, the British Rule in India would not be safe a month. The Legislature has therefore entrusted a modified power of this sort to the Executive as one of its permanent prerogatives, but has carefully fenced it round so as to prevent the chance of abuse. Only the Supreme Government can exercise it at all, and the Supreme Government only by a formal act of the Governor-General in Council. The preamble further limits its application to purely political cases, affecting 'the due maintenance of the Alliances formed by the British Government with foreign powers, the preservation of tranquillity in the territories of native princes entitled to its protection, and the security of the British Dominions from foreign hostility and from internal commotion.'[1] Special provision is made for the good treatment of such prisoners. The law carefully demarcates their status from that of convicted persons, and terms their confinement not imprisonment, but 'personal restraint.' They enjoy an allowance from the Government. They have liberty to forward any representation or petition to the Governor-General in Council direct.[2] The officer in charge of such a State prisoner is bound to report to the head of the Government, whether the degree of confinement is such as might injure his health, and whether his allowance is adequate to support himself and his family, 'according to their rank in life.'[3] His property generally remains in his own hands or those of his family. But if Government finds it necessary to take charge of his estates, they are exempted from sale, whether in satisfaction of the demands of the land revenue or of the decrees of the Civil Court. They receive, in fact, all the protection accorded to property under the Court of Wards. The law takes ample precaution to prevent anything like an unnecessarily prolonged restraint. Every officer in charge of a State prisoner arrested by the Executive must report twice a year to the Head of the Government direct, 'on the conduct, the health, and the comfort of such State prisoner, in order that the Governor-General

[1] Regulation III. of 1818, Clause I.
[2] *Idem*, Clause V.
[3] *Idem*, Clause VI.

in Council may determine whether the orders for his detention shall continue in force, or shall be modified.'[1]

There can be little doubt that, had this Act been applied to the confederacy which the Campaign of 1858 and the subsequent inquiries disclosed, British India would have been spared the disastrous Frontier War of 1863. A few well-aimed arrests would have saved us nearly a thousand soldiers killed or wounded in the Ambeyla Pass, and many hundred thousand pounds. Even after that calamitous war, if the conspiracy which the State Trial of 1864 brought to light had been broken up by a vigorous use of the power of arrest by the Executive, we should in all probability have been spared the Campaign on the Black Mountain in 1868. But for reasons which I have dwelt on elsewhere,[2] the Indian Government is traditionally loath to recognise the political dangers which environ it, and which from time to time have imperilled its rule. The enormous stake which England has in India, and the millions sterling which British Capitalists have annually invested in railways, canals, and other reproductive works since the country passed under the Crown, would now render even a temporary displacement of our authority an appalling calamity. Costly wars on our Frontier, severe judicial sentences within our territory, had alike failed to put down the fanatical confederacy; and in 1868 the Government at length resolved to vigorously enforce its power of arresting the offenders.

This measure could be carried out without risk of injury to the innocent, and without popular agitation of any sort. Lists of the leading traitors in each District

[1] Regulation III. of 1818, Clause III.

[2] Annals of Rural Bengal, vol. i. p. 241, 4th ed.

had for several years been in the hands of the authorities, and the Hindu population looked on their arrest as a thing sooner or later to be expected. The most conspicuous preachers of sedition were apprehended; the spell which they had exerted on their followers was broken; and by degrees a phalanx of testimony was gathered together against those more secret and meaner, although richer, traitors who managed the remittances, and who, like the Army Contractor in the Trial of 1864, carried on a profitable business as underwriters of treasonable risks.

The last seven years have brought forth five great State Trials in Districts many hundreds of miles apart, but all connected with the self-same conspiracy. Indeed, each case seems inevitably to give rise to a whole crop of others, and it is impossible to unearth a traitor in one Province without coming on subterraneous passages leading to half a dozen nests of treason in distant parts of the country. The evidence recorded in the Ambálla Trial of 1864, rendered necessary the Patna Trial of 1865; and the cumulative facts then disclosed led to a host of new arrests, with the Maldah Trial of September 1870, the Rájmahal Trial in October of the same year, and the great Trial which has just now condemned another batch of Fanatics to transportation for life (1871). I do not wish to stir up popular indignation either against the convicted traitors, or against the numerous unhappy men under surveillance or restraint who have not yet been tried. Such cases are best left to the calm action of the law, and inflammatory incidents taken from the late Trials could do no good. But in order that the reader may understand what a Wahábi Trial means, how obstinately it is fought out by highly paid English barristers who catch at every quibble or legal straw, and how costly it is to the State, I shall give a few bare facts touching the last one. The preliminary investigation employed the Magistrate's Court about two months. The subsequent trial before the Sessions' Judge occupied a month and three weeks, during which the Court sat thirty-eight days, examined 159 witnesses, and went over a vast mass of documentary evidence written in many languages. From the Sessions' Judge it has now come to the High Court in Calcutta; and when it will end, or how much more it will cost, no prudent man would venture to predict.

It may well be imagined how such a Trial, dragging its weary length for close on a whole year, in the midst of a fanatical populace, stirs up the hatred of zealots against our rule. Just before it was coming on in the High Court, a Musalmán assassin stabbed the Chief Justice of Bengal on the steps of his own Tribunal. As I write these lines, the passions, both of English and Musalmáns, have reached a heat such as has happily been unknown since the Mutinies. Indian society has again grown electric, and it will require no small wisdom and firmness to prevent an explosion. I cannot, however, let this second edition go forth without bearing testimony against anything like an alarmist or sensational mode of dealing with the evil. The Courts of British India are perfectly strong enough to put down the crimes of British India. It may perhaps be deemed expedient to strengthen the powers of arrest already in the hands of the Executive; but this is a question for calm deliberation by the Legislature, not for rash resolve by an indignant community, still within the shadow of its great and sudden loss.

Meanwhile these arrests, and the judicial proceedings which followed, have at length aroused the Muhammadans to the danger which the Fanatic Sect is bringing upon their whole community. They have determined to separate themselves from the schismatical conspiracy by a formal public act. Each section of them has accordingly published the authoritative Decisions[1] of its Law Doctors on Holy War, and proclaimed its disapproval of the Wahábi sedition. These curious documents form the subject of the next Chapter. The Fanatical Conspiracy itself gives signs of at last breaking down. The most active of its heads are under restraint, and the remainder know that the same fate awaits them if they again make themselves conspicuous. But the armed Colony, although insignificant in itself, still survives on the Frontier, and may at any time become the nucleus of a great religious coalition. This very morning[2] on which I finish the present Chapter, an Indian Newspaper generally most trustworthy in its statements announces another raid upon the Black Mountain. On the 4th June a tribe came down in force, and burnt three villages, in spite of a stubborn defence by the inhabitants.[3] Within four hours of the news of the outrage, the 3d Panjáb Infantry and a detachment from the 4th Panjáb Cavalry were on the march from our nearest military station, with what result is not reported. Nor have the causes, whether fanatical or otherwise, yet been ascertained. Only this is known, that for weeks the whole Press of British India has been discussing the probabilities of another Afghán War; and should any such trial be in store for us, it will be no small danger averted if the Wahábi conspiracy within our territory can be first stamped out.

[1] *Fatwas.*

[2] Simla, June 14, 1871. (First edition.)

[3] *Pioneer*, June 12, reached Simla, June 14.

## CHAPTER III.

### THE DECISIONS OF THE MUHAMMADAN LAW DOCTORS.

THE Wahábis have not been allowed to spread their network of treason over Bengal without some opposition from their countrymen. Besides the *odium theologicum* which rages between the Muhammadan Sects almost as fiercely as if they were Christians, the presence of Wahábis in a district is a standing menace to all classes, whether Musalmán or Hindu, possessed of property or vested rights. Revolutionists alike in politics and in religion, they go about their work not as reformers of the Luther or Cromwell type, but as destroyers in the spirit of Robespierre or Tanchelin[1] of Antwerp. As the Utrecht clergy raised a cry of terror when the last-named scourge appeared, so every Musalmán priest with a dozen acres attached to his mosque or wayside shrine[2] has been shrieking against the Wahábis during the past half century. Between 1813 and 1830 no Wahábi could walk the streets of Mecca without danger to his life, nor indeed, up to the present hour, without risk of insult and violence.

[1] 'His sect was the one true Church. He was encircled by a body-guard of three thousand armed men; he was worshipped by the people as an angel, or something higher; they drank the water in which he had bathed.'—Milman's History of Latin Christianity, vol. v. p. 389, ed. 1867.

[2] Generally a tomb with a little land, or a mango grove, left *in pios usus*.

In India, as elsewhere, the landed and clerical interests are bound up by a common dread of change. The Muhammadan landholders maintain the cause of the Mosque, precisely as English landholders defend the Established Church. Any form of Dissent, whether religious or political, is perilous to vested rights. Now the Indian Wahábis are extreme Dissenters in both respects; Anabaptists, Fifth Monarchy men, so to speak, touching matters of faith; Communists and Red Republicans in politics. From the first their hand has fallen heavily on any Muhammadan so criminal as to differ from their views. In 1827–30, it was against an obdurate Musalmán Governor of Peshávar, quite as much as against the Hindu Sikhs, that their divine Leader turned his arms. In the peasant rising around Calcutta in 1831, they broke into the houses of Musalmán and Hindu landholders with perfect impartiality. Indeed, the Muhammadan proprietors had rather the worst of it, as the banditti sometimes gave salvation to the daughter of an erring co-religionist by forcibly carrying her off, and appropriating her to one of the robber chiefs. The official description of the Sect, fifteen years afterwards,[1] 'as a gathering of eighty thousand men asserting complete equality among themselves, and drawn from the lower classes,' would make any landed gentry in the world indignantly uncomfortable.

Nor, indeed, would a religious Jacquerie of this sort find favour with the fundholding community, or with any section of the comfortable classes. In Bengal, however, one entire trade (and a very rich and powerful one) has been steadily on their side. The skinner and leather-worker ranks at the very bottom of the Hindu com-

[1] By Mr. Dampier, Commissioner of Police for Bengal, in letters already cited.

munity. He lays impious hands on the carcase of the sacred animal, the cow, and profits by its death. He is a man unclean from his birth, an outcast from decent society, whom no wealth or success in his detested vocation can raise to respectability. This degraded position he accepts like a true Hindu, with an untroubled mind. No exertions can raise him in the social scale; so he never makes the attempt. No honesty or sobriety could win for him the regard of his neighbours; so he lives quite happy without it. If the cows belonging to the village die in adequate numbers to supply him with leather, good and well. If they show a reluctance to mortality, he stimulates the too tardy death-rate with a little arsenic. A man of this hopeless sort never rises above petty retail dealings, and the wholesale hide trade (one of the great Indian staples) has thus fallen into the hands of Musalmán merchants. The Muhammadan knows nothing of the scruples which so powerfully influence the Hindu with regard to trafficking in the skin of the sacred animal. The Musalmán hide-merchants have therefore the monopoly of the export trade, and compose one of the richest classes of the native mercantile community. But they are looked upon with hatred and abhorrence by the Hindus. This detestation they pay back in kind. They well know that if the Bráhman ever gets the upper hand for a moment, they will be the first spoil of the Infidel. They accordingly regard the Infidel Hindu as a fair spoil for themselves, and form the wealthiest and most powerful contributors to the Wahábi sect, whose very *raison d'être* is to wage war upon the Unbeliever.

But it is not to any single class, however rich or powerful, that the Wahábis owe their strength. They appeal boldly to the masses; and their system, whether of religion or of politics, is eminently adapted to the hopes and fears of a restless populace. Among them, as I have already stated, and again cheerfully declare, are thousands of sincerely pious men, who look upon self-abnegation as the first duty of life. This element leavens the whole lump, and gives a respectability, and almost a sanctity, to the worldly-minded majority. The Wahábi of the nobler sort knows no fear for himself, and no pity for others. His path in life is clear, and neither warnings nor punishments can turn him to the right hand or the left. There is at present in one of the Bengal jails a venerable white-haired Musalmán, of blameless life in all respects, with the exception of his being a bitterly persistent traitor. For nearly thirty years his treason has been known to the authorities, and he himself has been perfectly aware that his practices were thus known. He was formally warned in 1849, again in 1853, again in 1857, and in 1864 he was publicly called up in Court before the Magistrate to receive a final admonition. To all such counsels he turned a deaf ear, and in 1869 he had to be placed under personal restraint. Such a case is very difficult to deal with. Government naturally shrinks from proceeding to extremities against a man really conscientious and devout according to his lights; and perhaps all that can be done is to prevent his injuring others by a mild personal restraint.

The Wahábi vocation is by no means a smooth or an easy calling. In the first place, all who profess the new faith must yearly part with a good deal of money in support of it. For those who take a more active part and join the Camp on the Frontier, a worse fate remains. I have never read anything more piteous than the evidence given by such recruits during the late trials. The summing up of the Judges shows that the Wahábi preachers have drafted away to certain slaughter batch after batch of deluded youths, generally under twenty, and often without the consent of their parents, from nearly every District of Eastern Bengal. That they have introduced misery and bereavement into thousands of peasant families, and created a feeling of chronic anxiety throughout the whole rural population, with regard to their most promising young men. No Wahábi father who has a boy of more than usual parts or piety, can tell the moment at which his son may not suddenly disappear from the hamlet. Of the youths thus spirited away, by far the greater portion perish by pestilence, famine, or the sword. The few who return, bring back a firm conviction that they have been used as tools and cast aside when they were no longer required. Here is the story of one of those who suffered least:—'I am a disciple of the Patna Khalíf. When I was ten or twelve years of age, I went to Rámpur Bauleah (a town in Lower Bengal, not far from the native village of the witness) to study under him. The masters were planning a Holy War, and arranging for sending money and men to support it. When about fifteen years old, I also was sent to join the Holy War. We went by Patna and Dehli (a distance of about two thousand miles to the Frontier Camp). I stayed with the Khalíf at Patna for one night. At Dehli my companions went on, but I remained there to study under a religious teacher for a year and a half. Thereafter, a detachment passing through Dehli to join the Frontier Camp, I went with them as far as Gujrat. Some time after, another detachment having arrived, I went with them to the mountains, where I had been assured that the Imám Sayyid Ahmad had reappeared. I there found between eight and nine thousand men assembled, the leader being the master with whom I had studied as a boy of twelve (and who had now succeeded to the Patna Caliphate). Here I discovered that no Divine Leader had appeared, and that all was a sham. I and others were angry, and returned to Dehli. Afterwards an Arab came to Dehli, who assured us that the Divine Leader had appeared at Sittána, and persuaded me again to go and join the Holy War. When I arrived, I asked about the appearance of the Divine Leader, but could get no answer. I soon discovered that we had been again deceived; and on some British Troops coming to attack us, I escaped to Dehli. Afterwards I returned to my own home.'[1]

This is the story of a well-cared-for recruit, who in the end came off unhurt. Into the more miserable narratives of those who fell victims to pestilence, exposure, or poverty by the way, I do not propose to enter. A single returned Crescentader from the Frontier does more to ruin the Wahábi cause in a District than a State Trial. His presence acts as a perpetual dis-illusionment to the fanatical youths who press forward for enlistment, and many even of the really sincere Wahábis have become willing to listen to any interpretation of the law which frees them from the obligation to rebel.

Such interpretations have fallen on Bengal thick as Autumn leaves during the past few years. The Wahábi preachers, not content with swaying the fanatical masses, attempted to bind the burden of Holy War upon the shoulders of all ranks of their countrymen. Now it is a

[1] Abridged from the evidence of Muhammad Abbás Alí before the Judge of Dinájpur, 15th August 1870. I have avoided as much as possible the use of proper names.

very trying position for a man in easy circumstances to be compelled either to join in a dangerous conspiracy or to be denounced as an Apostate. For a time it was possible to contribute without much personal danger; but since the enforcement of the power of arrest by the Executive, abetment of rebellion has become a perilous game, of which only the more bigoted consent to take the risks. Subscriptions from wealthy widows have come in more sparingly, and men with a stake in the country shirk giving money for the Holy War at the Mosques. On the other hand, the more fanatical of the sect have blazed up in denunciations against those who, from fear of an Infidel Government, have abandoned the cause of the Faith. They stigmatize the deserters as cowardly and self-seeking, and indignantly reject the Laodicæan casuistry by which the comfortable classes strive to serve both God and the World.

For a time the well-to-do Muhammadans bore these reproaches in silence. But they had the whole vested interests of the Musalmán clergy to back them, and by degrees drew out a learned array to defend their position. They began to contest the Wahábi doctrine of Holy War on first principles, and to deny that they were under any obligation to wage war against the Queen. During the past few years, a whole phalanx of *Fatwas* or Authoritative Decisions have appeared on this side. Even the three great High Priests[1] at Mecca have been enlisted to liberate the Indian Musalmáns from the dangerous duty of rebelling against an English Queen.

To arrive at this satisfactory result demanded no

[1] The Mufti of the Hanafí sect, the Mufti of the Sháfi'í sect, and the Mufti of the Málikí sect. The fourth orthodox sect, the Hanbalí, are few in number in Mecca, and have no Mufti there.

small amount of lawyer-like acumen. The plain meaning of the Kurán is, that the followers of Islám shall reduce the whole earth to obedience, giving to the conquered the choice of conversion, of a submission almost amounting to slavery, or of death. The Kurán was written, however, to suit, not the exigencies of a modern nation, but the local necessities of a warring Arabian tribe in its successive vicissitudes as a persecuted, an aggressive, and a triumphant sect. The rugged hostility and fanaticism of the Kurán have been smoothed down by many generations of scholiasts and interpreters; and from its one-sided, passionate bigotry, a not unsymmetrical system of civil polity has been evolved. Many of the Prophet's precepts on Holy War have, however, found their way unaltered into the formulated Muhammadan Law. The great Indian text-book, the Hidáyah, devotes a special chapter to the duty and incidents of waging war against the Infidel, and this necessity has been strongly insisted upon by the chief Indian Doctors of Muhammadan Law. But in the discussions which have lately agitated the Musalmáns, very little has been said about the Kurán; and all parties have by tacit consent removed the question from the text of the sacred book to the jurisdiction of the Canon Law, which has been based upon it.

It is a matter of congratulation, both for the Musalmáns and ourselves, that these Decisions have been on the side of peace and loyalty. It is scarcely possible to exaggerate the dangers which might have resulted had these *Fatwas* been in favour of rebellion. The mere fact of the question having been raised at all, reveals the perilous ground upon which our supremacy in India is based: for it should never be forgotten that such Decisions, when opposed to the Government, have given rise to some of the most obstinate and bloody revolts that the world has seen. Even Akbar was nearly hurled from the height of his power by a Decision of the Jaunpur lawyers declaring that rebellion against him was lawful. The great military revolt in Bengal followed, and from that time several of the landholders in the Lower Provinces had to be treated as feudatories rather than as subjects. During the Mutinies of 1857, the first act of a Musalmán rebel, when he proclaimed the Dehli Rule in a city, was to call on some Muhammadan local saint for a *Fatwa* declaring Holy War against the English. In Europe, whenever the Porte wished to hurl its hordes against Bulgaria or other of the Christian Provinces lying on the Austrian Frontier, it heated the fanaticism of its troops to the proper warmth by a Decision of the Law Doctors on the duty and rewards of War against the Infidel. We Christians did much the same thing, and the flagging zeal of the Holy Roman Empire was lashed into activity by a very similar set of stimulants during the later Crusades. In Muhammadan countries, such religious declarations in favour of exterminating those who differ in faith occupy the rank of high Legal Decisions, and collections of them were easily procurable in Constantinople when I was there in 1867. In more recent times, both the Pasha of Egypt and the Sultán of Turkey himself have been forced into disastrous hostilities against religious insurgents who believed that the Commander of the Faithful had departed from the sacred law, and that it was their duty to destroy the apostate and his armies. It is an auspicious circumstance, therefore, that the very District[1] which levelled the *Fatwa* of rebellion against the greatest Musalmán monarch whom India pro-

[1] Jaunpur.

duced, has also furnished the Law Doctor whose Decision is most strongly opposed to waging war against the British Power.[1]

I propose briefly to state the various solutions of the question at which the two recognised Musalmán Sects, the Shias and Sunnis, have within the past few months arrived.

The Shias take up a ground of their own touching the duty of the Faithful to wage war against the Queen, as they do on all other points. It is the view of a sect who have never been very numerous in India, and who have been accustomed to persecutions under the orthodox Muhammadan Governments such as no British ruler would sanction. The little Persian Pamphlet[2] which they put forth some time ago on the subject of Holy War, would carry no weight with the Sunnis, who form nine-tenths of the Muhammadans in India. But as the authoritative declaration of a distinguished Doctor of the Shiah Law, in consultation with the chief authorities among his sect, including a great spiritual functionary of the ex-King of Oudh, it deserves a notice. The Shias, although not a numerous body, have contributed some of the greatest names to the history of India; and in the discussion regarding the duty of rebellion which has been going on in every District during the last four years, they have made themselves distinctly heard.

The key-note to the Shiah faith is the belief in the twelve Imáms, an inspired Apostolic descent from the Prophet of God. One Imám yet remains to complete the august line, but is at present hidden away from sinful

[1] Maulaví Karamat Alí, in a Lecture delivered before the Muhammadan Literary Society of Calcutta, 23d November 1870.

[2] 'On the word Jihád as it is understood and believed by the Shiah Sect,' by Munshi Amír Alí Khán Bahádur. Calcutta, 1871.

mortals. Till his appearance the world travaileth and goeth in pain, and the Faithful suffer tribulation at the hands of heretical Sunnis, Christians, and others. But there will come a great Epiphany or shining forth of the Promised One, when all wrongs shall be righted, and all men converted to the true knowledge of God. Till then, the Shiah tract argues that it would be vain to attempt by mortal efforts, or rebellions, or wars, to bring about that great consummation. It denounces as schismatics all who disagree with this view. 'Now-a-days, such of the depraved and seditious as are ignorant of the precepts of Muhammad[1] and strangers to truth, with vain desires improperly indulge in foolish talk about the meaning and duty of Holy War.' 'In this country, Hindustán, only two sects among the followers of Islám have proved orthodox—the Shias and Sunnis. The remaining tribes of Musalmáns, whether they belong to the sect of Wahábis or to the sect of those who are styled Faráizís, etc., are such as have wandered from the right path, and cannot be trusted.' After explaining the three meanings of the word *Jihád*,[2] the pamphlet lays down seven conditions which must be fulfilled in order that *Jihád*, in its meaning of Holy War against the Infidel, may become lawful. 'First, when the rightful Imám is present, and grants his permission. Second, when arms and ammunition of war and experienced warriors are ready. Third, when the *Jihád* is one against mutineers and enemies of God.[3]

[1] Shúra.

[2] (1.) *Jihád fi-'lláh*, diligence in the adoration of God, who is glorious. (2.) *Jihád ba Nafs-i-Ammára*, the conquering of inordinate appetites, and bringing them under the control of reason, so as to make them yield to acts of devotion, deter them from unlawful pursuits, and keep a watch over the misspending of time. (3.) *Jihád fi-'d-dín*, or Holy War against the Infidel, as authorised by Muhammadan Law.

[3] Harb-i-Káfir.

Fourth, when he who makes Holy War is in possession of his reason, when he is not a lunatic or a man of impaired senses, and when he is neither sick, nor blind, nor lame. Fifth, when he has secured the permission of his parents. Sixth, when he is not in debt. Seventh, when he has sufficient money to meet the expenses of his journey and of the inns by the way, and to pay for the maintenance of his family.'

Putting aside the expediency of waging war against the Queen, and without any reference to the chances of its failure or success, the great Shiah condition required for a Holy War is the presence of the Imám. Now, hitherto this Divine Leader has withheld his face from mortal men. He has not yet condescended to appear and lead the armies of the Faithful. Till his shining forth, any attempt at Holy War is presumptuous and sinful. 'When that innocent Apostle,' says the Pamphlet, 'shall appear, is known only to the all-knowing God, and to no one else. To commit bloodshed, except under the leadership of that Imám in person, is strictly forbidden by the Shiah law. Those are the rebels and sinful ones who would revolt without the Divine sanction of the Apostle.'

The last sentence is a hit at the Sunnis, who have again and again declared Holy War without the Rightful Leader, and with whom the Shias have a long account of persecution and martyrdom to settle. The arrow is barbed by a very innocent, and on the surface a very charitable, reference to the ultimate conversion of the whole world to Islám, but a reference which would give great pain to the rival sect. The Indian Sunnis and Shias alike believe in the eventual triumph of the True Faith. But with a difference. The Sunnis hold that in the latter days they will carry out the injunction of the Prophet in its entirety, and subdue the whole world to Islám. The Shias, on the other hand, maintain that when that triumph comes, it will be achieved by an amalgamation (although a one-sided one) of the two great religions, Christianity and Islám. This dream of a universal fraternisation in the last days is common to all religions of the nobler type. The Hindus have a Book of the Future [1] which foretells a time when all men shall be of one religion and of one caste. Even the Vishnu Purána, compiled [2] amid the triumph of Hindu bigotry over Buddhism, admits that in the last Iron Age to which we have now come, men shall obtain the liberation of their souls, not in virtue of their religion or their race, but by purity of life and rectitude of action. The Shiah Musalmáns have also their millennium, and it is to be reached in association with the Christians, who will all become Shias, and probably through the blood of the Sunni heretics, who at first will refuse to accept the final Apostle. 'It is distinctly laid down in our Muhammadan Law,' the Pamphlet proceeds to say, 'that at the time when the above-named Imám shall appear, Jesus Christ (may safety attend him!) shall descend from the Fourth Heaven, and friendship, not enmity, shall exist between these two Great Ones.'

It is satisfactory to learn, therefore, that at least one small sect of our Muhammadan fellow-subjects are not bound by the first principles of their religion to rebel against the Queen. Whatever other Musalmáns may do, the handful of Shias in India declare that they will not compel us by force of arms to the disgraceful alternative of circumcision or slavery. But welcome as such an assurance may be, I cannot forget that the Shias

[1] Bhavishya Purána.

[2] Circ. A.D. 1050.

admit a principle of religious compromise,[1] which rather weakens the strength of any engagement they may make with us infidels. All over the world, except in Persia, they have been a persecuted people; and, like other hunted sects, have developed a system of casuistry to save their bodies by what seems to strangers something very like a denial of their faith. Thus a Shiah pilgrim may pass himself off as a Sunni at Mecca, without peril to his soul. When put to straits by their persecutors, they smooth over or deny the peculiarities of their belief. In extreme peril, as lately in Syria, and from time to time in India, this Law of Pious Fraud has allowed them to denounce their most cherished tenets, and even to curse the Twelve Imáms. But under the British Power they have been protected from persecution, and from the temptation to insincerity to which persecution gives rise. Their present declaration of the non-obligation to rebel is spontaneous, and it is well that such a declaration has been put on record. It comes to us stamped with the highest authority which the Shias can give to any document, and will be permanently binding on the whole sect. Even without a formal pledge of this sort, they are naturally loyal; for they know that if either the Hindus or the Sunni Muhammadans ever get the upper hand in India, the days of tribulation for the Shias will begin. Nor would the Sunnis, in their hour of victory, forget that the Legal Decision, which declares that the ultimate triumph of Islám is to be shared by Muhammadans and Christians alike, issued from the palace of the ex-King of Oudh. His late Majesty's loyalty, and that of the party which he represents, will henceforth shine with redoubled lustre, when they remember the darts which this Shiah pamphlet has

[1] Takíyah, literally 'guarding oneself,' 'pious fraud.'

left rankling in the hearts alike of their Wahábi and of their Sunni countrymen.

I now pass to the Formal Decisions of the greater sect. The Sunnis, as they are the most numerous class of Indian Musalmáns, so they have of late been the most conspicuous in proclaiming that they are under no religious obligation to wage war against the Queen. To that end they have procured two distinct sets of Legal Decisions, and the Muhammadan Literary Society of Calcutta has summed up the whole Sunni view of the question in a forcibly written pamphlet. I would commend this little work to those who doubt the intellectual acumen of the Bengáli Musalmáns, or their capacity for judicial posts under our Government. It is a triumph of legal subtlety, for it contains two separate sets of syllogisms starting from contradictory premises, yet arriving at the same desirable conclusion. The Law Doctors of Northern Hindustán set out by tacitly assuming that India is a Country of the Enemy,[1] and deduce therefrom that religious rebellion is uncalled for. The Calcutta Doctors declare India to be a Country of Islám,[2] and conclude that religious rebellion is therefore unlawful. This result must be accepted as alike satisfactory to the well-to-do Muhammadans, whom it saves from the peril of contributing to the Fanatic Camp on our Frontier, and gratifying to ourselves, as proving that the Law and the Prophets can be utilised on the side of loyalty as well as on the side of sedition.[3]

Unfortunately, however, it is not the well-to-do Musal-

[1] *Dár-ul-Harb*, literally House of Strife. [2] *Dár-ul-Islám*.

[3] The Pamphlet is entitled, 'Abstract of Proceedings of the Muhammadan Literary Society of Calcutta, on Wednesday, 23d November 1870. Being a Lecture by Maulaví Karamat Alí of Jaunpur on a question of Muhammadan Law, involving the Duty of Muhammadans in British India towards the Ruling Power.' Calcutta, 1871.

máns, but the fanatical masses, who stand in need of such Decisions. The powers of arrest granted by Regulation III. of 1818, to enable the Executive to deal with widely spread treason, such as has during the past twenty years been smouldering in Bengal, and from time to time bursting out in conflagrations on our Panjáb Border, have at length rendered any dabbling in rebellion a most perilous pastime. The comfortable classes, even among the conspirators, are now glad of a pretext to wash their hands of the business. Such men will welcome the Legal Decisions as a door of escape out of a serious difficulty. They will not inquire too closely into their strict validity, but will accept them as an emollient salve for tender consciences, and refrain from troublesome questionings as to the composition of the agreeable medicament. From this point of view the Muhammadan Society of Calcutta has deserved well of its countrymen and of ourselves; and Maulavi Abd-ul-Latíf Khán Bahádur, its Secretary, merits especial thanks. Whatever view a Sunni Musalmán may take as to the religious status of India under our Rule, he will find that according to that view he is not compelled to rebel against our Government. Does he hold that India is still a Country of Islám? Let him turn to page 6, and he will learn that to wage war against the Queen is therefore unlawful. Does he hold that India has become a Country of the Enemy? Let him turn to the long footnote on page 11, and he will find that for that very reason rebellion is uncalled for.[1]

[1] Here and elsewhere throughout this Chapter, I have made use of some articles which I lately put forth in the Calcutta *Englishman*, to whose successive editors, during the past seven years, I owe my acknowledgments for the courtesy with which they have inserted my perhaps too frequent contributions, on what I conceive to be the wrongs and requirements of the Muhammadan community.

In the following remarks, therefore, I would disclaim any intention of underrating the service which Maulavi Abd-ul-Latíf has done by the publication of this Tract. But it would be a political blunder for us to accept without inquiry the views of the Muhammadan Literary Society of Calcutta as those of the Indian Musalmáns. Extreme zealots of the Wahábi sect cannot be expected to listen to reason of any sort, yet there is a vast body of pious Muhammadans, who would be guided by a really authoritative exposition of their Sacred Law.

Between a man's convictions and his actions there generally stretches a wide gap, especially when giving full effect to his views leads him into the perils of treason. But with good men there is a constant struggle to abridge this distance, and to make practice conterminous with belief. Hitherto such men, without being fanatical Wahábis, have simply accepted the obligation of Holy War as an unpleasant duty. It is they who have proved the mainstay of the Frontier Camp in money matters, and whom it is specially desirable to win over to the side of peace and loyalty. I propose, therefore, to scrutinise the Sunni Decisions with a view to ascertaining the effect which they will have on the more zealous Muhammadans; men with whom the sense of religious duty is the rule of life, and whose minds are uninfluenced either by fear of danger or by habits of prosperous ease. For it is no use shutting our eyes to the fact that a large proportion of our Muhammadan subjects belong to this class. During a third of a century they have kept on foot a rebel army, first against Ranjit Singh, and afterwards against ourselves as his successors. In the distant Province of Bengal they have equipped band after band for the Frontier Camp. Every village, indeed almost every family, has followed their example and contributed to the cost of the war. Our prison gates have closed upon batch after batch of unhappy misguided traitors; the Courts have condemned one set of ringleaders after another to lonely islands across the sea; yet the whole country continues to furnish money and men to the Forlorn Hope of Islám on our Frontier, and persists in its bloodstained protest against Christian Rule.

I am very sorry to say that the effect of the Decision of the Calcutta Society on this numerous and dangerous class will be simply *nil*. The Pamphlet, however, exhibits two distinct lines of argument against Holy War; one of them the view of the Society itself, the other the Formal Decisions of the Law Doctors of Northern India. These last are introduced only to be rebutted, but they had previously appeared in an independent form, and, as I shall presently show, have worked out a really authoritative argument from the Muhammadan Texts against rebellion.

In the first place, it is only due to the learned authors of the Pamphlet to state wherein their argument fails. Its object is to prove that India is a Country of Islám,[1] and that THEREFORE Religious Rebellion is unlawful for Muhammadan subjects. Significantly enough, the word THEREFORE is omitted in the fundamental statement of the question on page 1. Still more significantly, the two most important Decisions, that of the Mecca Doctors and of Maulavi Abd-ul-Hakk, confine themselves to affirming that India is a Country of Islám, and *most carefully avoid drawing the inference that rebellion is therefore unlawful.* The truth is, that, according to strict Muhammadan law, the opposite conclusion would be

[1] *Dár-ul-Islám.*

correct, and the Mecca Doctors well knew this when they gave their decision. They affirm that India *is* a country of Islám, and leave it to the Faithful to conclude that for this very reason they ought to strive, by war or otherwise, to drive out the Infidels who have usurped the Government, and who in a hundred ways have interfered with the practices and procedure, both legal and religious, of the former Muhammadan rulers.[1]

The Pamphlet argues that India is still a Country of Islám because it was so under the Muhammadan Rule, and that, although now conquered by an infidel race, yet the three conditions under which it would have become a Country of the Enemy (*Dár-ul-Harb*, literally House of Strife) do not apply to it. These three conditions were laid down by the greatest authority of the Muhammadan Law, Abu Hanífa. The Tract quotes them, however, not from one of the older and universally received works, but from the *Fatáwi-i-Alamgírí* of the reign of Aurangzeb. This latter text materially differs from the earlier works; and it is an unquestionable fact that the conditions, as laid down by Abu Hanífa and by the old authoritative law-books, *do* apply to India, and that, according to the orthodox doctrine, India *is* a Country of the Enemy. I place the two enunciations of the Law in parallel columns, and leave the reader to judge for himself:—

THE THREE CONDITIONS UNDER WHICH A COUNTRY OF ISLAM BECOMES *Dár-ul-Harb*, OR A COUNTRY OF THE ENEMY.

| According to the Pamphlet, p. 3, citing the *Fatáwi-i-Alamgírí*. | According to the *Sirajiyah Imadiyah*, and all texts older than the *Fatáwi-i-Alamgírí*. |
|---|---|
| (1.) When the Rule of Infidels is openly exercised, *and the ordinances of Islám are not observed.* | (1.) When the Rule of Infidels is openly exercised. |

[1] See Appendix I., the Mecca Decision.

| | |
|---|---|
| (2.) When it is in such contiguity to a country which is *Dár-ul-Harb* that no city of *Dár-ul-Islám* intervenes between that country and *Dár-ul-Harb.* | (2.) When it is in such contiguity to a *Dár-ul-Harb* that no *Dár-ul-Islám* lies between it and the said *Dár-ul-Harb, so that no help can be brought from the Dár-ul-Islám to that country.* |
| (3.) That no Musalmán is found in the enjoyment of religious liberty, nor a *Zimmí* (an Infidel who has accepted the terms of permanent subjection to Musalmán Rule) under the same terms as he enjoyed under the Government of Islám. | (3.) When neither Musalmáns nor Zimmís enjoy the *Amán-i-áwwal* (a technical term which will be explained hereafter).[1] |

These three conditions, as laid down in the older and more authoritative texts, apply to India.[2] With regard to the first of them, it will be seen that the *Fatáwi-i-Alamgírí* adds certain words which I have italicised, and for which there is no authority in the earlier law-books, which cite direct from Abu Hanífa. The first condition as authoritatively laid down is simply that 'the rule of the Infidels be openly exercised;' and this condition most unquestionably applies to India at the present hour. With regard to the second condition, the Pamphlet makes an omission as unwarranted as the addendum to the preceding one. According to the orthodox texts, *India is a Country of the Enemy because no intervening country exists between it and England* (the *Dár-ul-Harb* in question), *which can send help to India to prevent*

[1] For this collection of Texts, as also for several of the *Fatwas*, and many of the arguments contained in my examination of the Sunni Pamphlet, I am indebted to Professor Blochmann of the Muhammadan College, Calcutta, a gentleman who will yet be recognised in Europe as one of the brightest ornaments of Indian scholarship.

[2] Abu Hanífa held that the whole of the three conditions above mentioned had to be fulfilled in order that a Country of the Faithful should lapse into a state of a Country of the Enemy. His two disciples, the *Sáhibán*, *i.e.* Imám Muhammad and Imám Yusuf, held that the existence of one of the conditions sufficed. The Calcutta Sunnis rightly support the authority of Abu Hanífa against the *Sáhibán* (p. 4 of the Pamphlet); but I shall show that all the three conditions are now fulfilled in India, so that both according to Abu Hanífa and his disciples the Country has become a *Dár-ul-Harb*.

*its lapsing into the state of Dár-ul-Harb.* When England conquered India, the road between the countries was the *sea*, and it is clearly laid down in the *Hamawi* and *Tahtawi* that *the sea is Dár-ul-Harb.* Consequently, on the original and still the principal highway from India to England, there is no Country of the Faithful which could send help to Hindustán. That Cabul, a Country of the Faithful, borders on India, has nothing to do with the question; for Abu Hanífa's condition only refers to such a land as intervening on the road between the two countries, and able to assist in preventing the one of them from lapsing into a Country of the Enemy. Now no one will pretend that Cabul lies on the route between England and India, or has any power to send aid to the Muhammadan subjects in the latter.

But the most serious misinterpretation lurks in the Pamphlet's rendering of the third condition. The whole force of this condition turns upon the meaning of the term *Amán-i-áwwal*, which the Tract translates as 'religious liberty.' But these words totally fail to give a correct idea of what is meant. '*Amán*' literally signifies *security*, and the meaning of *Amán-i-áwwal* is distinctly laid down in the *Jámi'-ur-rumúz* as implying the whole religious security and full status which the Muhammadans *formerly* enjoyed under their own Rule. This authority, which the Calcutta Sunnis themselves will not venture to dispute, says that a Country becomes a Country of the Enemy, (1) when Musalmáns and Zimmís (*i.e.* the Infidels subject to them) enjoy only such *Amán* (religious status) as the Infidels choose to grant; and (2) when the full religious status formerly enjoyed under their own Government, and the religious status which they, as the then ruling race, granted to the Infidels subject to them, no longer exist. Now it is perfectly clear that both these clauses apply to India at present. The *Amán*, or religious status, which the Muhammadans now enjoy, is entirely dependent on the will of their Christian rulers, and they enjoy it only in such a degree as we choose to grant. This degree falls far short of the full religious status which they formerly possessed. The British Government taxes the Muhammadans, and applies the taxes to the erection of Christian Churches, and the maintenance of a Christian Clergy. It has substituted Englishmen for the Muhammadan governors whom it found in charge of the Districts and Provinces. It has formally abolished the Musalmán Judges and Law Officers.[1] It allows pork and wine to be openly sold in the market-places. It has introduced English into the Courts. It has superseded the whole Muhammadan procedure and criminal law. It has afforded protection to unhappy fallen women by Act XIV. of 1868.[2] It makes no provision such as a king is bound to make, according to the Musalmán Code, for seeing that the people attend the mosques and perform their religious duties. It must be remembered that the civil and religious law of Islám, and the civil and religious status of Musalmáns, are inseparably mixed up. The stamps required by our Courts on a plaint, our statutes of limitation, the orders by our Judges to pay interest upon money found to be due, and our entire system of legal procedure and religious toleration, are opposed to the Muhammadan law, and are infringements of the *Amán*, or status, which our Musalmán subjects enjoyed under their own rulers. Nor has the religious status of the *Zimmís*, or Christian and other

[1] Kázis, by Act XI. of 1864, on which more hereafter.

[2] The Indian Contagious Diseases Act.

Infidel subjects of the Muhammadan Empire of India, undergone less change. The Christian *Zimmís* are there no more a subject people, but conquerors and governors. The Hindu *Zimmís* no longer pay the poll-tax;[1] and we have interfered with their religious usages in a hundred ways, such as doing away with Trial by Ordeal, abolishing widow-burning, ignoring their system of caste, and giving a legislative recognition to converts to Christianity. In short, the *Amán-i-áwwal*, or former status both of Muhammadans and of *Zimmís*, has been totally altered; and according to the third condition also of Abu Hanífa, India has become a Country of the Enemy (*Dár-ul-Harb*).

The question has been settled over and over again, as a few analogous cases will show. Greece was a Country of Islám so long as it remained under the Turk. But since it shook off the Musalmán yoke half a century ago, it has always been held to be a Country of the Enemy, notwithstanding the Muhammadan population which remained in it. The same remark applies to several of the Danubian Provinces, the South of Spain, and every country in which a similar revolution of Government has taken place. The *Mabsút* of Imám Muhammad, Abu Hanífa's celebrated disciple, thus lays down the law: 'When a Country of Islám falls into the hands of the Infidel, it remains a Country of Islam *if the Infidels retain Muhammadan Governors and Muhammadan Judges,*[2] *and do not introduce their own Regulations.*' We have not retained Muhammadan Governors; we have abolished the Muhammadan Law Officers; we have introduced our own Regulations; and India has, according to the doctrine followed by the great majority of Indian Musalmáns, ceased to be a Country of Islám.

[1] Jizya. [2] Kázis.

The Wahábis start with the declaration that India has become a Country of the Enemy, and from this they deduce the obligation of Holy War against its rulers. The Calcutta Pamphlet denies the first position, and asserts that India has not become a Country of the Enemy, but still continues a Country of Islám. It has failed, however, to make out its case, and it will produce no effect whatever on the great body of earnest Muhammadans whom it is so important to win over to our side. The Law Doctors of Upper India have argued from quite a different basis. They do not deny the Wahábis' first position, that India has ceased to be a Country of Islám, but they deny that the obligation to Holy War follows therefrom.

This, I believe, is the true solution of the difficulty. Had India remained a Country of Islám, as the Mecca Law Doctors insidiously try to make out, a large portion of the orthodox sect would have deemed themselves bound to rebel. If India were still *de jure* a Country of Islám, this portion of our Musalmán subjects would feel compelled to rise against us, and to make it a Country of Islám *de facto*. It is written in all the law books: 'If Infidels press hard or occupy a town in a Country of Islám,[1] it is absolutely incumbent[2] on every Muhammadan man, woman, and child to hurt and drive away the Infidel Ruler.' This is so established a rule, that the King of Bokhára was compelled by his subjects to declare Holy War against the Russians as soon as they entered the Country of Islám. Indeed, if India were still a Country of the Faithful, every day some ground of rebellion would arise. Our religious toleration would itself constitute a capital crime. For example (and not to mention graver

[1] *Bilád-ul-Islám.* [2] *Farz-'ain.*

causes of offence), the Muhammadan texts lay down that if the Ruler or King of a Country of Islám does not look after the maintenance and spread of the True Faith, rebellion against him becomes lawful. In the reign of Akbar, who modified the Muhammadan law in a spirit of toleration towards his Hindu subjects, Formal Decisions commanding rebellion were published, and led to bloody insurrections. Much more would rebellion now be incumbent (if India had not ceased to be a Country of Islám) in the case of the English, who have interfered in a hundred points with the Muhammandan Code, extirpated the Musalmán Law Officers, and abolished the whole Islámitic Procedure. I therefore view with extreme suspicion the decision of the Doctors at Mecca, that stronghold of fanaticism and intolerant zeal, when they declare that India is a Country of Islám, but who, instead of deducing therefrom, as the Calcutta Muhammadan Literary Society infer, that rebellion is *therefore* unlawful, leave it to their Indian co-religionists to draw the opposite conclusion,—namely, *that rebellion is therefore incumbent.*

Nevertheless there is a class of Indian Musalmáns who would not draw this inference. To them it will be a comfort that so respectable a body as the Muhammadan Society of Calcutta has formally declared, by the mouths of eminent Doctors of the Law,[1] that India is still a country of the Faithful, and that rebellion is therefore uncalled for. For in the Muhammadan as in the Christian community, an endless conflict of doctrine goes on. To enable the reader to enter into the feelings of this class,

[1] Maulaví Karamat Alí of Jaunpur; Sheikh Ahmad Effendi-el-Ansárí; Maulaví Abd-ul-Hakím; besides a Muhammadan gentleman of high English education and keen practical intelligence, Maulaví Abd-ul-Latíf Khán Bahádur.

I give below[1] the speech of a venerable Sheikh at the Meeting on whose proceedings the Pamphlet is based. The English are apt to misinterpret Indian affairs from a purely European point of view. They will find that their Asiatic subjects, who are six times more numerous than the whole population of the British Isles, can twist European politics with equal ignorance and with equal hardihood to suit Indian exigencies.

The Calcutta Decision, although erroneous, will be acceptable to many easy-going well-to-do Muhammadans.

[1] 'Sheikh Ahmad Effendi-el-Ansárí (a respectable resident of Medina, and a descendant of Abu Ayyub-el-Ansárí, one of the Companions of the Prophet), who has for several days been staying in this City, next rose and said that he was not a Member of the Society. But as he had the good fortune of being present at the Meeting, he would ask permission to be allowed to say a few words, as the discussion was on a very important subject, involving the propriety or otherwise of a great many acts performed by Muhammadans, both secular and appertaining to Divine Worship, and had also a personal bearing on his own conduct in coming to this Country, and residing here for several years.

'The President replied that the Meeting would listen to him with great pleasure, and would feel highly obliged to him, and that whatever he would say would be considered of great value.

'The venerable Sheikh thereupon said, that before this he had travelled in many countries, and that he had been twice to Constantinople. The first time he went there was during the reign of the late Emperor, Sultán Mahmúd Khán; and on that occasion he stayed there for two years. The second time was after the accession to the throne of the present Sovereign, Sultán Abd-ul-Azíz Khán, when he remained there for fourteen months. He had also been to Egypt, Syria, and several cities in Asiatic Turkey, residing there for various periods; and this was his fourth visit to India. He had first come to this country about twenty-nine years ago, and remained at different places for nearly seven or seven and a half years. Thus he had been two and a half years at Dehli, and two years and nine months at Lucknow, during the reign of the late Amjud Alí Sháh; and while there he was all along the guest of the King, who was exceedingly kind, hospitable, and courteous to him. For two years he was at Haidrábád in the Deccan, and then proceeded to Baroda. From there he had proceeded to Afghánistán, where he continued travelling for four or four and a half years. His visit to Afghánistán was made in the company of the brother of Amír Dost Muhammad Khán of Cabul, and during his residence at Cabul he had been a guest of the King. On two other occasions also he had come to India, but returned after staying only at Haidrábád in the Deccan, and in the Province of Sindh respectively. It was nearly a year since he had this time come to India, and he had been travelling through Bombay, Bhopál,

But the Authoritative Declaration of the Law Doctors of Northern India will prove of far wider use. It accepts the Wahábi position of India being a Country of the Enemy, and deduces by logical steps the duty of the existing Muhammadans to live as peaceable subjects. I give their decision, which is a technical matter, as an Appendix, and now briefly unfold the more interesting historical aspects of the case.

During the first half of the eighteenth century, precisely the same question arose as that which now agitates

Rámpur, Allahabad, Patna, Gaya, etc., and had lastly arrived at Calcutta. He had this time also been very hospitably received everywhere, especially by Her Highness the Begum of Bhopál and His Highness the Nuwáb of Rámpur, to whom particularly he could not sufficiently express his gratitude for their unbounded kindness and hospitality. The reasons of his giving the details of his travels was, that from this varied experience which he had the good fortune to acquire in his sojourn in so many different countries, especially during his four visits to India, he was in a position to support and verify all that had been said by the several speakers with reference to the particular subject before the Meeting, especially the statement of the Secretary as to the friendship between Her Majesty the Queen of England and His Majesty the Sultán of Turkey. In truth, there was a closer intimacy between the British Nation and the Sultán, than between the Sultán and any other Nation in the World. He, the speaker, remembered a very recent incident which strongly testified to the great sincerity existing between the British Nation and the Sultán. A short time ago the Khedive of Egypt showed a spirit of insubordination and disloyalty towards the Sultán. There was every probability of the occurrence of serious events, and the Sultán ultimately sent a menacing and peremptory Firmán to the Khedive, a compliance with which alone could induce the Sultán to overlook the misconduct of the Khedive. The Khedive hesitated to comply with the requisitions of his Liege Sovereign, and very likely he would not have obeyed the Mandate at all. But before doing anything, he communicated to the British Consul-General the Message that the Sultán had sent, and waited for advice. This was given at once. The British Consul-General informed the Khedive that he had received instructions from the British Ministry, that unless the Khedive obeyed the Imperial Mandate, the Consul's orders were to telegraph to the British fleet at Athens to proceed to Alexandria at once. On hearing this the Khedive gave way, and all thoughts of rebellion vanished from his mind. He at once complied with the peremptory and humiliating conditions of the Mandate, and returned to obedience and loyalty. This shows the extreme degree of cordiality and friendship of the British Nation with the Sultán. They had already fought with a Foreign Enemy of the Sultán, and now they expressed their readiness to fight against an Internal Enemy who had assumed the attitude of a rebel. Although the Sultán was, even single-handed, more the Indian Musalmáns in the second half of the nineteenth. The Marhattá Infidels had overrun the Muhammadan Empire of India. Provinces which had formerly been ruled over by Musalmáns or by Hindu deputies, according to the Muhammadan Law, were seized by an Unbelieving Dynasty. Among the more devout Musalmáns, the question of their status under the conquerors, and of their obligation to rebel against them, immediately arose. It was decided that, inasmuch as the Marhattás satisfied themselves with taking one-fourth[1] of the revenue, with-

than equal to the task of bringing the Khedive to his senses, yet the British Nation did not like that he should be put to so much trouble and vexation. It is worthy of notice that they were at the same time on terms of friendship with the Khedive of Egypt. But this was because he enjoyed the position of the Sultán's Lieutenant, and they disregarded his friendship in a matter where the Sultán's interests were concerned. In short, had they not shown their readiness to fight against the Khedive, it would have been no matter of surprise if the latter had ventured to measure his strength with his Liege Sovereign; and the gentlemen present could well conceive the calamities of such an internal conflict. Owing to the promptness shown by the British Government, both the Sultán and the Khedive escaped the evil consequences of War. Is there a greater enemy to Islám than one who would like to wage war against such sincere friends of the Sultán of Islám? Again, as to British India being *Dár-ul-Islám*. Besides the Authorities already quoted by the speakers at this Meeting, a *Fatwa* had already been delivered by the most learned and pious men of the two Holy Cities of Mecca and Medina. This he considered was more than sufficient for the purpose; for those venerable learned men have pronounced British India to be *Dár-ul-Islám*, after a thorough investigation into all the circumstances of this country.

'On the strength of this *Fatwa*, a native of Arabia comes to this country without any hesitation, and remains here as long as he chooses without applying for or obtaining any guarantee from the British Rulers for civil and religious liberty. Besides this, about twenty-nine years ago, when he first came to this country, there existed hundreds of most learned and pious Muhammadans in Dehli and Lucknow, with all of whom he was on terms of intimacy, but he never heard any one of them calling India *Dár-ul-Harb*. All of them treated this country as *Dár-ul-Islám*, and all the injunctions necessary in *Dár-ul-Islám* were observed here. It was within the speaker's experience that in those days were observed, as at present, the Prayers of Friday and the two 'Ids. No change had taken place which could take away the character of *Dár-ul-Islám* from this country.' The learned Sheikh had kept such good company on his travels, that he was quite oblivious to what was going on among the masses of the Indian Musalmáns.

[1] *Chauth*.

out further interfering with the actual administration, India still remained a Country of Islám. They left the Muhammadan Governors of Provinces untouched. They maintained the Muhammadan Judges and Law Officers[1] undisturbed. On the demise of a Musalmán Governor, a new ruler of the same religion was appointed. Indeed, the confirmation of his hereditary successor was considered a matter of right upon payment of a present to the distant Marhattá Court. The following is the Decision which the greatest authority of that time gave forth :[2]—'Now let us suppose that a Country of Islám has fallen into the hands of Infidels, who, however, permit the Muhammadans to say their Friday and 'Id Festival prayers ; who maintain the law of Islám, and appoint *Kázis* to carry it out according to the wishes of the Musalmáns, but in which, nevertheless, the Muhammadans have to ask the Infidels to appoint [the Musalmán] Governors. Such countries unhappily exist in our time, where Muhammadan Governors are appointed by Infidels, and where the Friday and 'Id Festival prayers are still said. For the Infidel [Marhattás] have taken possession of some of our Provinces. It is therefore needful for every Muhammadan to know what the law says in such a case.

'The truth is, that if such a Muhammadan Province falls into the hands of the Infidels, it continues a Country of the Faithful, because no Country of the Enemy is adjacent to it, and because the law of the Infidels is not introduced, and because the Governors and the Judges

[1] *Kázis.*

[2] I have again to express my acknowledgments to Professor Blochmann for this *Fatwa*. He copied it from an Arabic work by Kázi Muhammad Ala, son of Maulaví Sheikh Alí, son of Kázi Muhammad Hamíd, son of Maulaví Takí-ud-dín Muhammad Sabir, a descendant of Omar of Tharnuah. It is entitled *Ahkám-ul-arází*, or Orders on Land Ṭenures, and deals chiefly with real property in a *Dár-ul-Islám*.

are Muhammadans, who decide according to the law of Islám, and because even the Infidels themselves refer all matters to the Muhammadan law, and the Musalmán Law Officers pass sentence on the Infidels.'

Not one of the reasons here assigned for India continuing a Country of the Faithful holds good at the present day. The early servants of the East India Company perfectly understood their position; and when they first took over the Provinces, they left the Muhammadan Administration absolutely undisturbed. They retained the Muhammadan code as the law of the land, appointed Muhammadan Law Officers to carry it out, and in the smallest matter, as in the greatest, acted merely *in the name* of the Muhammadan Emperor of Dehli. Indeed, so afraid was the East India Company of assuming the insignia of sovereignty, that long after its attempts to govern the country through the Musalmáns had broken down, in consequence of the indescribable corruption of the Muhammadan administration, it still pretended to be the Deputy of a Musalmán Monarch. It is a matter of history how this pretence in the end sunk into a contemptible farce, and how we struck coins [1] in the name of the King of Dehli, while our Resident was paying the poor pensioner a monthly allowance for his table expenses.

As Indian history has hitherto been generally written by persons [2] who have never set foot in India, it would be

[1] Bearing after 1773 the following superscription, slightly changed according to the name of the Emperor: 'The King Sháh'alam, the Defender of the Faith of Muhammad, the shadow of the grace of God, has struck this coin to be current through the seven climes.' On the reverse: 'Struck at Murshidabád in the 19th year of the auspicious accession.'

[2] With the conspicuous exception of Marshman's and Meadows Taylor's excellent volumes. Mountstuart Elphinstone does not come down to the period in question.

unfair to expect that the meaning of this strange moderation on the part of the East India Company should be understood in England. The truth is, that had we hastened by a single decade our formal assumption of the sovereignty, we should have been landed in a Muhammadan rising infinitely more serious than the mutinies of 1857. The whole status of the Musalmáns would have been suddenly changed. We should have been in the position of an Infidel Power who had seized and occupied a Country of Islám. The great majority of the Indian Musalmáns would have deemed it their absolute duty to rebel; for, as I have already shown, the first obligation 'of every man, woman, and child,' in such a case, 'is to hurt and drive away the Infidel Ruler.'[1]

The admirable moderation of the East India Company's servants, and their determination to let the Muhammadan Power expire by slow natural decay, without hastening its death a single moment, averted this danger. India passed from a Country of Islám into a Country of the Enemy[2] by absolutely imperceptible gradations. After many years' study of the Imperial and District Archives, I find myself unable to place my finger on any given year or decade of years as that in which the change was effected. We got rid of the subordinate Muhammadan Governors long before we touched the nominal supremacy of the Muhammadan Emperors. Long after that nominal supremacy had become a farce, and indeed up to 1835, our coinage still issued in his name.[3]

[1] *Mabsút* of Imám Muhammad.

[2] *i.e.* from a *Dár-ul-Islám* to a *Dár-ul-Harb*.

[3] The Company's Rupee of 1835, of 180 grains Troy, was the first one bearing the head of the British Sovereign and the name of the East India Company.

Even after we thus ventured to impress the British Sovereign's effigy on our coin, we maintained much of the Muhammadan Procedure along with the Muhammadan Court Language. These in their turn slowly disappeared. But it was not till 1864 that we took the bold step, and in my opinion the unwise step, of doing away with the Muhammadan Law Officers by an Act[1] of the Legislature. This Law put the last touch to the edifice of the new Empire of India as a Country of the Enemy, the rebuilding of which had been wisely spread over one hundred years (1765 to 1864). While the Muhammadan Rule thus imperceptibly disappeared, a new set of obligations on the part of our Musalmán subjects was springing up. Before India had passed into a Country of the Enemy, the duties incumbent upon the Muhammadans in a Country of Islám had faded away. One of the first of these duties, as I have already said, is rebellion against an Infidel Conqueror. But when the change has been finally accomplished, a new set of obligations comes into play. The position of the Muhammadans wholly alters. The existing generation is not responsible for the change; and instead of being the owners of the country suddenly deprived of their rights and bound to regain them, they have become what is technically called *mustámin*, or seekers for protection. As such, they obtain from their English Rulers a certain amount of their civil and religious privileges (*Amán*). Not indeed their former complete status[2] under Muhammadan Rule, but sufficient for the protection of their lives and property, and the safety of their souls. No interference is made with their private prayers or

[1] Act XI. of 1864.

[2] The *Amán-i-áwwal* of the *Sirajiyah*, *Imadiyah*, and all other texts older than the *Fatáwi-i-Alamgírí*.

public worship, and their religious lands and foundations are respected. In return for this fair amount of religious and civil liberty (*Amán*), they accept, as their forefathers during the past fifty years have accepted, the position of subjects. The same authorities which would have formerly compelled them as Muhammadans in a Country of Islám to resist an Infidel Invader, now bind them, as subjects of a Country of the Enemy, to adhere to their engagements with, and to live peaceably under, an Infidel Ruler.

The duty of waging war has thus disappeared. The present generation of Musalmáns are bound, according to their own texts, to accept the *status quo.* They are not responsible for it, and they are forbidden, in the face of God's providence, and with regard to the immense perils in which a revolt would involve the True Faith, to have recourse to arms. They are compelled to adhere to the mutual relation which has sprung up between the rulers and the ruled, and to perform their duties as subjects so long as we maintain their status (*Amán*) sufficiently intact to enable them to discharge the duties of their religion.

If, however, their English Governors should infringe the tacit agreement by interfering with the prayers, or the public worship, or other lawful ceremonies of their Muhammadan subjects, or with the erection of Mosques, or with pilgrimage, or with the adoration of saints, or with the domestic law of Islám, then rebellion would be lawful. If, under such circumstances, rebellion, although lawful, were impracticable, then wholesale emigration or Flight (*Hijra*) becomes incumbent on every devout Musalmán. The various conditions under which such Flight is necessary are laid down by Sháh Abd-ul-Azíz, and are given in all Law Books.

In my next Chapter I shall show that we have lately trenched perilously near upon these conditions. For the object of this little book is not merely to explain the duties of our Muhammadan subjects to their rulers, but to impress upon the rulers their duty to the ruled. The Decision of the Law Doctors of Northern India, which I have expanded historically in the foregoing pages, will carry weight with the very classes whose goodwill it is important to conciliate. But it will carry weight with them only so long as we respect their rights and religious privileges. The Wahábis to a man, and a large proportion of the devout Musalmáns, believe India to be now a Country of the Enemy. But the more sensible majority of them, while sorrowfully lamenting its lapsed state, are willing to accept the duties belonging to that condition. The whole Kurán is based upon the conception of the Musalmáns as a conquering, and not as a conquered people. As already explained, however, the Kurán was long ago found inadequate to the necessities of Civil Polity, and a system of Canon and Public Law has been developed from it to suit the exigencies of Musalmán nations. It is hopeless to look for anything like enthusiastic loyalty from our Muhammadan subjects. But we can reasonably expect that, so long as we scrupulously discharge our obligations to them, they will honestly fulfil their duties in the position in which God has placed them to us.

The more acute among the Law Doctors long ago detected the coming change in the status of the Musalmáns of India,—the change which has now become an accomplished fact. From time to time Decisions have appeared, which show that, in spite of the cautious timidity of the East India Company, the revolution did not go on unperceived. One of these Decisions declared that India would remain a Country of Islám only so long as the Muhammadan Judges, whom we have abolished, continued to administer the Law. But perhaps the two most important were those of Sháh Abd-ul-Azíz, the Sun of India, and of his nephew Maulavi Abd-ul-Haí. As we gradually transferred the administration to our own hands, pious Musalmáns were greatly agitated touching the relation which they should hold to us. They accordingly consulted the highest Indian authorities on the point, and both the celebrated men above mentioned gave forth responses. Here are their decisions word for word:—

'When Infidels get hold of a Muhammadan country,' Abd-ul-Azíz declared, 'and it becomes impossible for the Musalmáns of the country, and of the people of the neighbouring districts, to drive them away, or to retain reasonable hope of ever doing so; and the power of the Infidels increases to such an extent, that they can abolish or retain the ordinances of Islám according to their pleasure; and no one is strong enough to seize on the revenues of the country without the permission of the Infidels; and the (Musalmán) inhabitants do no longer live so secure as before; such a country is politically a Country of the Enemy (*Dár-ul-Harb*).'

When we consolidated our power, the decisions of the Doctors became more and more distinct as to India being *Dár-ul-Harb.* Maulavi Abd-ul-Haí, who belongs to the generation after Abd-ul-Azíz, distinctly ruled as follows: 'The Empire of the Christians from Calcutta to Dehli, and other countries adjacent to Hindustán proper (*i.e.* the North-West Provinces), are all the Country of the Enemy (*Dár-ul-Harb*), for idolatry (*Kufr* and *Shirk*) is everywhere current, and no recourse is made to our holy law. Whenever such circumstances exist in a country, the country is a *Dár-ul-Harb*. It is too long here to specify all conditions; *but the opinions of all lawyers agree in this, that Calcutta and its dependencies are the Country of the Enemy (Dár-ul-Harb)*.'

These Decisions have borne practical fruit. The Wahábis, whose zeal is greater than their knowledge, deduce from the fact of India being technically a Country of the Enemy, the obligation to wage war upon its rulers. The more enlightened Musalmáns, while sorrowfully accepting the fact, regard it not as ground of rebellion, but as a curtailment of their spiritual privileges. For example, in a Country of Islám, where the full religious status exists, the Friday Prayer is absolutely incumbent. In India not only do many devout Muhammadans refrain from this service, but some of the mosques refuse to allow its performance. Thus the two most eminent Musalmáns of Calcutta in their respective walks of life, the late head Professor[1] of the Muhammadan College, and the late Chief of all the Muhammadan Law Officers,[2] refrained from saying the Friday Prayer. They accepted the position of India as a Country of the Enemy as a curtailment to this extent of their religious privileges. But they lived loyal subjects to, and honoured servants of, the British Government. Many Muhammadans who acknowledge the lapsed state of India, do not go so far as to deny themselves the consolations of the Friday Service. A still greater number would break their connection with the Wahábi party if they could see their way to doing so

[1] Maulaví Muhammad Wajíh.

[2] The Kázi-'l-Kuzát Fazl-ur-Rahmán.

without peril to their souls. The Formal Decisions lately issued by the Law Doctors of Northern India, with the historical amplification now set forth, will give peace to thousands of devout men.

It may seem that a cold acquiescence in our rule is but a meagre result from the discussions which have so long agitated the Muhammadan community. But such an acquiescence is the utmost that the intolerant spirit of Islám will permit to a really sincere disciple. Absolutely conscientious men, however, form a minority among Musalmáns as among Christians, and an established Government has always the worldly-minded on its side. No young man, whether Hindu or Muhammadan, passes through our Anglo-Indian schools without learning to disbelieve the faith of his fathers. The luxuriant religions of Asia shrivel into dry sticks when brought into contact with the icy realities of Western science. In addition to the rising generation of sceptics, we have the support of the comfortable classes; men of inert convictions and of some property, who say their prayers, decorously attend the mosque, and think very little about the matter. But important as these two sections of the Muhammadans may be from a political point of view, it has always seemed to me an inexpressibly painful incident of our position in India that the best men are not on our side. Hitherto they have been steadily against us, and it is no small thing that this chronic hostility has lately been removed from the category of an imperative obligation. Even now the utmost we can expect of them is non-resistance. But an honest Government may more safely trust to a cold acquiescence, firmly grounded upon a sense of religious duty, than to a louder-mouthed loyalty, springing only from the unstable promptings of self-interest.[1]

[1] If Government deemed it prudent to put the case to the Muhammadan Law Doctors in a really crucial shape, the following question would permanently bind them down to one side or the other. Such a proceeding happily does not seem called for at present; but in event of its ever becoming needful to make use of a public Test of Loyalty, this would be the best form for it:

QUESTION.

Learned Men and Expounders of the Law of Islám!
What is your opinion in the following matter:—

In the case of a Muhammadan Ruler attacking India while in the possession of the English, is it the Duty of the Muhammadans of that country to renounce the *Amán* of the English, and render help to the Invader?

## CHAPTER IV.

### WRONGS OF THE MUHAMMADANS UNDER BRITISH RULE.

THE Indian Musalmáns, therefore, are bound by their own law to live peaceably under our Rule. But the obligation continues only so long as we perform our share of the contract, and respect their rights and spiritual privileges. Once let us interfere with their civil and religious status (*Amán*), so as to prevent the fulfilment of the ordinances of their Faith, and their duty to us ceases. We may enforce submission, but we can no longer claim obedience. It is the glory of the English in India, however, that they have substituted for the military occupation of all former conquerors, a Civil Government adapted to the wants and supported by the goodwill of the people. Any serious wrong done to the Muhammadans would render such a Government impossible. Even minor grievances attain in their case the gravity of political blunders,—blunders of which the cumulative effect, according to the law of Islám, would be to entirely change the relation of the Musalmáns to the ruling power, to free them from their duty as subjects, and bind them over to treason and Holy War.

Of such blunders the Indian Government has, in my humble opinion, been more than once guilty. But before pointing out what I conceive to be our shortcomings, I beg it to be distinctly understood that my remarks refer only to those Muhammadans who peaceably accept the British Rule. The foregoing Chapters establish the two great facts of a standing Rebel Camp on the Frontier, and a chronic conspiracy within the Empire. The English Government can hold no parley with traitors in arms. Those who appeal to the sword must perish by the sword. Herr Teufelsdröckh's simile of the Alpine hamlet, Peace established in the bosom of Strength, applies in a nobler sense to the Indian Empire; and the first moment that the English in that country cease to be able, from financial or from any other reasons, to go to war upon a just cause, they had better take shipping from the nearest ports.

With regard, also, to the traitors within our territory, justice must have free course; but justice tempered with mercy, and mitigated by a knowledge of the not ignoble motives which lead men, sincerely good according to their lights, into treason. The powers of arrest granted by the Legislature to the Executive enable the Government to deal with the evil. The ringleaders suffer the penalty of personal restraint, without obtaining the glory of a public appearance on behalf of their faith. Even those sentenced to transportation for life by the Courts are treated with contemptuous leniency by the Government, being generally returned in a few years to the Muhammadan community, as apostates to the Wahábi cause. Any attempt to stamp out the conspiracy by wholesale prosecutions would fan the zeal of the fanatics into a flame, and array on their side the sympathies of all devout Musalmáns. The distempered class must be segregated without the slightest feeling of resentment, and indeed with the utmost gentleness, but with absolute strength.

But while firm towards disaffection, we are bound to see that no just cause exists for discontent. Such an inquiry would with more dignity have been conducted before pressure had been brought to bear from without. Concessions made when confronted by a great conspiracy, have small pretension to generosity or gracefulness. But if in any matter we have hitherto done injustice to the Muhammadans, it would be mischievous vanity to allow considerations of this sort to delay our doing justice now. The British Government of India is strong enough to be spared the fear of being thought weak. It can shut up the traitors in its jails, but it can segregate the whole party of sedition in a nobler way—by detaching from it the sympathies of the general Muhammadan community. This, however, it can do only by removing that chronic sense of wrong which has grown up in the hearts of the Musalmáns under British Rule.

For there is no use shutting our ears to the fact that the Bengal Muhammadans arraign us on a list of charges as serious as was ever brought against a Government. They accuse us of having closed every honourable walk of life to professors of their creed. They accuse us of having introduced a system of education which leaves their whole community unprovided for, and which has landed it in contempt and beggary. They accuse us of having brought misery into thousands of families, by abolishing their Law Officers, who gave the sanction of religion to the marriage tie, and who from time immemorial have been the depositaries and administrators of the Domestic Law of Islám. They accuse us of imperilling their souls, by denying them the means of performing the duties of their faith. Above all, they charge us with deliberate mālversation of their religious foundations, and with misappropriation on the largest scale of their educational funds. Besides these specific counts, which they believe susceptible of proof, they have a host of sentimental grievances, perhaps of little weight with the unimaginative British mind, but which not less in India than in Ireland keep the popular heart in a state of soreness to the Rulers. They declare that we, who obtained our footing in Bengal as the servants of a Muhammadan Empire, have shown no pity in the time of our triumph, and with the insolence of upstarts have trodden our former masters into the mire. In a word, the Indian Musalmáns arraign the British Government for its want of sympathy, for its want of magnanimity, for its mean malversation of their funds, and for great public wrongs spread over a period of one hundred years.

How far these charges are true, how far they are inevitable, I propose at some length to inquire. But I beg the reader to bring to this examination of our conduct towards the Muhammadans at large, a mind free from any petty resentment against the section of them whose misdeeds the foregoing chapters have recited. Insurrection and fanatical ebullitions are the natural incidents of an alien Rule; and so long as the English remain worthy of keeping India, they will know how to deal alike with domestic traitors and with frontier rebels. For my own part, once I have opened the case for the Muhammadan community, I shall make no further reference to these misguided Wahábis. But in order that I may afterwards keep silence about them, I shall here quote certain statements by the two Englishmen who, of all the present generation, are most competent to pronounce on the connection between Musalmán grievances and Musalmán seditions. In India, the line between sullen discontent and active disaffection is a very narrow one, and our inattention to the wants of the peaceable Muhammadans in Bengal has enlisted their sympathies on the side of a class whom they would otherwise shrink from as firebrands and rebels.

The officer in charge of the Wahábi prosecutions[1] lately wrote: 'I attribute the great hold which Wahábi doctrines have on the mass of the Muhammadan peasantry to our neglect of their education.' He then goes on to show how the absence of a career under our Rule affects, in an equally pernicious way, the higher classes, for whose instruction our schools do make some slight provision. 'In the Ambálla Trial will be found a case exactly in point. 'Osmán Alí, a man personally known to me, says: "About three years since I had occasion to go to Jessor. There I met the Chief Bailiff of the Judge's Court. He asked me of my state. I said my fortunes were much broken. He answered, 'You are an educated man, and ought not to be in distress. If you like what I am going to tell you, you will do well.' I asked, 'What is it?' He replied, 'Take your Scriptures in your hand, and go into the neighbouring Districts, and preach the injunctions of your creed to the people; and when you see likely men, induce them to go on the Crescentade.' Accordingly I preached throughout the neighbouring Districts. Many people gave me money." Here is a man who, from what I have known of him, I believe preached partly from belief and partly for money. The whole country has been overrun by such men. They have excited the peasantry, and the Ambeyla campaign has shown us that they are not to be despised, and that the timid Bengali will, under certain conditions, fight as fiercely as an Afghan.'

[1] Mr. James O'Kinealy, C.S.

'Is it any subject for wonder,' writes a still higher authority,[1] 'that they have held aloof from a system which, however good in itself, made no concession to their prejudices, made in fact no provision for what they esteemed their necessities, and which was in its nature unavoidably antagonistic to their interests, and at variance with all their social traditions?

'The educated Muhammadan, confident in his old training, sees himself practically excluded from the share of power and of the emoluments of Government which he hitherto had almost monopolized, and sees these and all the other advantages of life passed into the hands of the hated Hindu. Discontent—a feeling if not of actual religious persecution, yet of neglect on account (indirectly) of his religious views—has filled the minds of the better educated. Their fanaticism, for which ample warrant can always be found in the Kurán, has been hotly excited, until at last there is danger that the entire Muhammadan community will rapidly be transformed into a mass of disloyal ignorant fanatics on the one hand, with a small class of men highly educated in a narrow fashion on the other, highly fanatic, and not unwarrantably discontented, exercising an enormous influence over their ignorant fellow-Muhammadans.'

But, indeed, from the highest official to the lowest (and no one has penetrated into the wrongs of the Musalmáns more deeply than the present Viceroy), there is now a firm conviction that we have failed in our duty to the Muhammadan subjects of the Queen. A great section of the Indian population, some thirty millions in number,

[1] Mr. E. C. Bayley, C.S.I., Secretary to the Government of India in the Home Department, to whose scholarly sympathies the Musalmáns owe a debt of gratitude.

finds itself decaying under British Rule. They complain that they, who but yesterday were the conquerors and governors of the land, can find no subsistence in it to-day. Any answer based on their own degeneracy is a *petitio principii*, for their degeneracy is but one of the results of our political ignorance and neglect. Before the country passed under our rule, the Musalmáns professed the same faith, ate the same food, and in all essentials lived the same lives, as they do now. To this day they exhibit at intervals their old intense feeling of nationality and capability of warlike enterprise; but in all other respects they are a race ruined under British rule.

For this decay we are not entirely to blame. The Musalmáns can no longer, with due regard to the rights of the Hindus, enjoy their former monopoly of Government employ. This ancient source of wealth is dried up, and the Muhammadans must take their chance under a Government which knows no distinction of colour or creed. As haughty and careless conquerors of India, they managed the subordinate administration by Hindus, but they kept all the higher appointments in their own hands. For example, even after the enlightened reforms of Akbar, the distribution of the great offices of State stood thus:—Among the twelve highest appointments, with the title[1] of Commander of more than Five Thousand Horse, not one was a Hindu.[2] In the succeeding grades, with the title of Commander of from Five Thousand to Five Hundred Horse, out of 252 officers, only 31 were Hindus under Akbar. In the second next reign, out of 609 Commanders of these grades, only 110 were

[1] *Mansab.* See a very interesting but all too brief Pamphlet by Prof. Blochmann, 'The Hindu Rajas under the Mughul Government.' Calcutta, 1871.

[2] Under the reign of Sháhjahán. It should be remembered that these Military Titles were held by the Officers of the Civil Administration.

Hindus; and even among the lowest grades of the higher appointments, out of 163 Commanders of from Five Hundred to Two Hundred Horse, only 26 were Hindus.

It would be unreasonable for the Muhammadans to expect any such monopoly of offices under the English Government. But this is not their petition and complaint. It is not that they have ceased to retain the entire State Patronage, but that they are gradually being excluded from it altogether. It is not that they must now take an equal chance with the Hindus in the race of life, but that, at least in Bengal, they have ceased to have a chance at all. In short, it is a people with great traditions and without a career. When such a people have co-religionists in India numbering thirty millions of men, it becomes a question of not less importance to their rulers than to themselves to know what to do with them.

The greater part of the peasant population throughout Eastern Bengal is Muhammadan. In those districts of overwhelming rivers and boundless swamps, the aborigines were never admitted into the respectable Hindu community. The Aryan migration southwards had not penetrated in sufficient strength into the seaboard and Deltaic tracts, to thoroughly pound down in the Brahmanical mortar the earlier people of the soil. They accordingly remained beyond the pale of Hinduism, out-castes fishing in their remote estuaries, and reaping hazardous rice crops from their flooded lands, without social status or religious rites.[1] So impure are they, that a Bráhman of the highest caste cannot settle among them without taint,[2] and in a few generations his descendants cease

[1] I speak of the Districts south of Dacca and Vikrampur, the last great Brahmanical settlement in the Delta.

[2] This I ascertained by personal inquiry in Faridpur District, Báckarganj, and the Sundarbans.

to have the *jus connubii* with the Bráhman community a few days' journey to the north, from which they sprang.[1] The Muhammadans recognised no such distinctions. They came down upon the country, sometimes as military colonists, sometimes as heads of great reclamation enterprises in the Deltaic Districts. Even in an old settled District like Jessor, the earliest traditions begin with an enterprise of the latter sort.[2] As the primeval heroes of the inner parts of India slew monster beasts, quelled demon tribes, and hewed down the all-covering forest; so the first object that looms on the prehistoric horizon in Deltaic tracts, is the man who pushed forward tillage into regions formerly the prey of the sea.

The Musalmáns led several of these great land reclamation colonies to the southward, and have left their names in Eastern Bengal as the first dividers of the water from the land. The sportsman comes across their dykes, and metalled roads, and mosques, and tanks, and tombs, in the loneliest recesses of the jungle; and wherever they went, they spread their faith, partly by the sword, but chiefly by a bold appeal to the two great instincts of the popular heart. The Hindus had never admitted the amphibious population of the Delta within the pale of their community. The Muhammadans offered the plenary privileges of Islám to Bráhman and outcaste alike. 'Down on your knees, every one of you,' preached these fierce missionaries, 'before the Almighty, in whose sight all men are equal, all created beings as the dust of the earth. There is no God but the one God, and His

[1] On the ground that they have lived among, and in some cases acted as priests to, a low *chandál* population.

[2] Report on the District of Jessor, by Mr. James Westland, C.S.—by far the best account of an Indian Deltaic District that has yet appeared. Calcutta, 1871.

Messenger is Muhammad.' The battle-cry of the warrior became, as soon as the conquest was over, the text of the divine.

To this day the peasantry of the Delta is Muhammadan. So firmly did Islám take hold of Lower Bengal, that it has developed a religious literature and a popular dialect of its own. The *patois* known as Musalmán Bengáli is as distinct from the Urdu of Upper India, as Urdu is different from the Persian of Herát. Interspersed among these rural masses are landed houses of ancient pedigree and of great influence. Indeed, the remains of a once powerful and grasping Musalmán aristocracy dot the whole Province, visible monuments of their departed greatness. At Murshidabád a Muhammadan Court still plays its farce of mimic state, and in every District the descendant of some line of princes sullenly and proudly eats his heart out among roofless palaces and weed-choked tanks. Of such families I have personally known several. Their ruined mansions swarm with grown-up sons and daughters, with grandchildren and nephews and nieces, and not one of the hungry crowd has a chance of doing anything for himself in life. They drag on a listless existence in patched-up verandahs or leaky outhouses, sinking deeper and deeper into a hopeless abyss of debt, till the neighbouring Hindu money-lender fixes a quarrel on them, and then in a moment a host of mortgages foreclose, and the ancient Musalmán family is suddenly swallowed up and disappears for ever.

If an individual instance be demanded, I would cite the Rájás of Nagar. When the British first came into contact with them, their yearly revenues, after two centuries of folly and waste, amounted to fifty thousand pounds. From the pillared gallery of their palace the

Rájás looked across a principality which now makes up two English Districts. Their mosques and countless summer pavilions glittered round the margin of an artificial lake, and cast their reflections on its surface, unbroken by a single water-weed. A gilded barge proudly cut its way between the private staircases and an island in the centre covered with flowering shrubs. Soldiers relieved guard on the citadel; and ever, as the sun declined, the laugh of many children and the tinkling of ladies' lutes rose from behind the wall of the Princesses' garden. Of the citadel nothing now remains but the massive entrance. From the roofless walls of the mosque the last stucco ornament has long since tumbled down. The broad gardens with their trim canals have returned to jungle or been converted into rice-fields. Their well-stocked fish ponds are dank, filthy hollows. The sites of the summer pavilions are marked by mounds of brick dust, with here and there a fragmentary wall, whose slightly arched Moorish window looks down desolately upon the scene.

But most melancholy of all is the ancient Royal Lake. The palace rises from its margin, not, as of old, a fairy pillared edifice, but a dungeon-looking building, whose weather-stained walls form a fitting continuation to the green scum which putrefies on the water below.[1] The gallery is a tottering deserted place. The wretched women who bedeck themselves with the title of princesses[2] no more go forth in the covered barge at evening. Their luxurious zenana is roofless, and its inhabitants have been removed to a mean tenement overlooking a decayed stable-

[1] I describe the buildings and tank as I saw them in 1864. Since then, I hear that the latter has been cleaned, and the former fallen deeper into decay.

[2] *Ránís.*

yard. Of all the bygone grandeur of the House of Nagar, a little watercourse alone remains unchanged, holding its way through the dank solitudes in the same channel by which it flowed amid the ancient palaces, and reminding the spectator in its miniature way of the one immutable relic of antiquity in Rome:

> 'Ne ought save Tyber hast'ning to his fall
> Remaines of all: O world's inconstancie!
> That which is firme doth flit and fall away,
> And that is flitting doth abide and stay.'[1]

In a corner of the dilapidated palace, the representative of the race mopes away his miserable days, chewing drugged sweetmeats, and looking dreamily out on the weed-choked lake. If any statesman wishes to make a sensation in the House of Commons, he has only to truly narrate the history of one of these Muhammadan families of Bengal. He would first depict the ancient venerable Prince ruling over a wide territory at the head of his own army, waited on through life by a numerous household, with all the stately formality of an Eastern Court, and his death-bed soothed by founding mosques and devising religious trusts. He would then portray the half-idiot descendant of the present time, who hides away when he hears of an English shooting party in his jungles, and when at length dragged forth by his servants to pay the courtesy due to the strangers, lapses into a monotonous whimper about some tradesman's execution for a few hundred rupees which has just taken place in his palace.

I have dwelt at some length on the Musalmán peasantry and the Musalmán aristocracy of Bengal, in order to bring clearly before the English eye the class of people with whose grievances this chapter deals. I would further

[1] Spenser's Ruines of Rome, by Bellay.

premise that my remarks apply only to Lower Bengal, the Province with which I am best acquainted, and in which, so far as I can learn, the Muhammadans have suffered most severely under British Rule. I should be sorry to believe, or to convey to the reader the belief, that the following remarks were predicable of all the Muhammadans of India.

If ever a people stood in need of a career, it is the Musalmán aristocracy of Lower Bengal. Their old sources of wealth have run dry. They can no longer sack the stronghold of a neighbouring Hindu nobleman; send out a score of troopers to pillage the peasantry; levy tolls upon travelling merchants; purchase exemption through a friend at Court from their land-tax; raise a revenue by local cesses on marriages, births, harvest-homes, and every other incident of rural life; collect the excise on their own behoof, with further gratifications for winking at the sale of forbidden liquors during the sacred month of Ramazán. The administration of the Imperial Taxes was the first great source of income in Bengal, and the Musalmán aristocracy monopolized it.[1] The Police was another great source of income, and the Police was officered by Muhammadans. The Courts of Law were a third great source of income, and the Musalmáns monopolized them. Above all, there was the army, an army not officered by gentlemen who make little more than bank interest on the price of their commissions, but a great confederation of conquerors who enrolled their peasantry into troops, and drew pay from the State for them as soldiers. A hundred and seventy years ago it was almost impossible for a well-born Musalmán in Bengal to become poor; at present it is almost impossible for him to continue rich.

[1] This is subject to the explanation given further on.

The Muhammadan aristocracy, in short, were conquerors, and claimed as such the monopoly of Government. Occasionally a Hindu financier, and more seldom a Hindu general, came to the surface;[1] but the conspicuousness of such instances is the best proof of their rarity. Three distinct streams of wealth ran perennially into the coffers of a noble Musalmán House—Military Command, the Collection of the Revenue, and Judicial or Political Employ. These were its legitimate sources of greatness, and besides them were Court Services, and a hundred nameless avenues to fortune. The latter I have indicated at the beginning of the last paragraph, and of them I shall not further speak; but, confining myself to the three fair and ostensible monopolies of official life, I shall examine what remains of them to the Musalmán families of Lower Bengal under British Rule.

The first of them, the Army, is now completely closed. No Muhammadan gentleman of birth can enter our Regiments; and even if a place could be found for him in our military system, that place would no longer be a source of wealth.[2] Personally, I believe that, sooner or later, the native aristocracy of India must, under certain

[1] Whenever they did, great was the discontent among the Musalmáns. In the two best known cases, that of Rájá Todar Mall the Financier, and Rájá Mán Singh the General, formal deputations of remonstrance were sent to Court. In the case of Mán Singh, some of the Muhammadan Generals refused to serve under him in the Expedition against Rána Pratáb. I have already given the statistics of the Hindus who rose to conspicuous offices under the least bigoted of the Musalmán monarchs.

[2] A very few Muhammadan gentlemen hold commissions from the Governor-General, but, so far as I can learn, not one from the Queen. A native of India can only enter the Army as a private soldier, and the rare individual instances of men promoted from the ranks by a merely local commission form no exception to the rule. The single case of a Muhammadan obtaining even the honorary rank of Captain is Captain Hidáyat Alí, who was brought forward by Colonel Rattray during the mutiny,—a Muhammadan gentleman in every respect worthy to hold Her Majesty's commission, as I can by personal knowledge of himself and of his deeds attest.

restrictions, be admitted as Commissioned Officers in the British Army.[1] The supreme command of any regiment must always be vested in an Englishman. Indeed, great care would be required before the experiment can be entered upon at all; but the warlike peoples of Northern India could turn out under their own hereditary leaders, a light cavalry second to none in the world. Such employment would be eagerly sought after. No commissioned officer now-a-days expects to make a fortune by serving the Queen, and the Muhammadans are perfectly aware of this. But they covet the honours and decent emoluments of a military career, and bitterly feel that their hereditary occupation is gone.

The second support of the Musalmán aristocracy was the collection of the Land Revenue. This monopoly had its roots deep in the canon and public law of Islám. The payment of taxes was a badge of conquest; and to the conquerors accrued not only the revenue, but also the profitable duty of collecting it. It can never be too often insisted upon, however, that in India the relation of the conquerors to the native population was regulated rather by political necessity than by the Muhammadan Code. The haughty foreigners despised the details of collection, and left it to their Hindu bailiffs to deal directly with the peasantry. So universal was this system, that Akbar successfully defended the selection of a Hindu for his Minister of Finance by referring to it. On Todar Mall's appointment as Chancellor of the Empire, the Musalmán princes sent a deputation to remonstrate. 'Who manages your properties and grants of land?' replied the Emperor. 'Our

[1] Among the exponents of this view, I would particularly cite the most recent and the ablest—Captain Osborn of the Bengal Cavalry, in the columns of the Calcutta *Observer*.

Hindu agents,' they answered. 'Very good,' said Akbar; 'allow me also to appoint a Hindu to manage my estates.'

While the higher fiscal posts remained in the hands of the Musalmáns, the direct dealing with the husbandman was thus vested in their Hindu bailiffs. The Hindus, in fact, formed a subordinate Revenue Service, and took their share of the profits before passing the collections on to their Muhammadan superiors. The latter, however, were responsible to the Emperor, and formed a very essential link in the Muhammadan fiscal system. They enforced the Land Tax, not by any process of the Civil Courts, but by the sharp swords of troopers. Arrears were realized by quartering a marauding banditti upon a District, who harried the villages till the last penny was paid up. The husbandmen and Hindu bailiffs constantly tried to get off at less than the fixed sum; the superior Musalmán officers ceaselessly endeavoured to extort more than it.[1]

The English obtained Bengal simply as the Chief Revenue Officer of the Dehli Emperor. Instead of buying the appointment by a fat bribe, we won it by the sword. But our legal title was simply that of the Emperor's Diwán or Chief Revenue Officer.[2] As such, the Musalmáns hold that we were bound to carry out the Muhammadan system which we then undertook to administer. There can be little doubt, I think, that both parties to the treaty at the time understood this,[3] although the Grants and Treaties do not in my opinion bind us down.

[1] Curious illustrations of this perennial conflict occur in Mr. Westland's recent report on Jessor, and may be found in the rural archives of almost every District of Bengal.

[2] See the Firmáns of 12th August 1765, in Mr. Aitchison's Treaties, or in the Quarto Collection put forth by the East India Company in 1812, Nos. xvi. to xx.

[3] 'We took it under a kind of promise to carry on the Musalmán Rule as it then existed,' writes the Officer in charge of the Wahábi Prosecutions, 'and we did so.'

For some years the English maintained the Muhammadan officers in their posts; and when they began to venture upon reforms, they did so with a caution bordering upon timidity. The greatest blow which we dealt to the old system was in one sense an underhand one, for neither the English nor the Muhammadans foresaw its effects. This was the series of changes introduced by Lord Cornwallis and John Shore, ending in the Permanent Settlement of 1793. By it we usurped the functions of those higher Musalmán Officers who had formerly subsisted between the actual Collector and the Government, and whose dragoons were the recognised machinery for enforcing the Land-Tax. Instead of the Musalmán Revenue-farmers with their troopers and spearmen, we placed an English Collector in each District, with an unarmed fiscal police attached like common bailiffs to his Court. The Muhammadan nobility either lost their former connection with the Land-Tax, or became mere landholders, with an inelastic title to a part of the profits of the soil.

The Permanent Settlement, however, consummated rather than introduced this change. It was in another respect that it most seriously damaged the position of the great Muhammadan Houses. For the whole tendency of the Settlement was to acknowledge as the landholders the subordinate Hindu officers who dealt directly with the husbandmen. I have carefully gone over the MS. Settlement Reports of 1788–1790; and notwithstanding the clauses touching intermediate holders in the Code of 1793, it is quite clear to me that our Revenue Officers of those days had an eye to only three links in the previous system—the State, the local agent or landholder who collected direct from the peasantry, and the husbandman who tilled the soil. These were the three features of the former administration requisite to our new plan, and by degrees all the other links of the Muhammadan Revenue System were either extruded or allowed to drop out. For example, the provisions respecting the separation of Independent Talukdárs, or subordinate tenure-holders who held from the superior Musalmán lord by a perpetual lease, and paid their Land-Tax direct to the State, were in themselves fatal to the greatness of many a Muhammadan House. Such a family, although it might grant away part of its territory in permanent farm, always exercised a sort of jurisdiction over its subordinate holders, and, when occasion demanded, managed to extract cesses or benevolences, in short money in one form or another, from them. The officer who has studied the Permanent Settlement most minutely in connection with the present Muhammadan disaffection writes thus: 'It elevated the Hindu collectors, who up to that time had held but unimportant posts, to the position of landholders, gave them a proprietary right in the soil, and allowed them to accumulate wealth which would have gone to the Musalmáns under their own Rule.'[1]

This, then, is the first public wrong on which the Muhammadan aristocracy arraign the British Government. They assert that we obtained the Administration of Bengal from a Musalmán Emperor on the understanding that we would carry out the Musalmán system, and that as soon as we found ourselves strong enough we broke through this engagement. Our reply is, that when we came to look into the Muhammadan Administration of Bengal, we found it so one-sided, so corrupt, so absolutely shocking to every principle of humanity, that we should have been a disgrace to civilisation had we re-

[1] Mr. James O'Kinealy, C.S.

tained it. We can prove from the records of every District, that Revenue was the sole object of the Musalmán Government. 'Almost all the functions of Administration were heaped upon the Collectors of the Land-Tax, and they might do pretty much as they pleased so long as they discharged their revenue. The people were oppressed in order that the landholder might have his rent, and were plundered in order that the landholder's servants might become rich. Complaint against wrong was useless. The landholder or his officer had it entirely in his own option whether he should listen to it or not; and the complainant had very little chance of relief, for the oppressor was often the landholder's servant, and the plunderer, even if they took the trouble to trace him, would not find it difficult to make friends with his captors.'[1]

The truth is, that under the Muhammadans, government was an engine for enriching the few, not for protecting the many. It never seems to have touched the hearts or moved the consciences of the rulers, that a vast population of husbandmen was toiling bare-backed in the heat of summer and in the rain of autumn, in order that a few families in each District might lead lives of luxurious ease. It is only after we had begun to break away from the system which we had virtually engaged to uphold, that the existence of the People discloses itself. The greatest wrong which we did to the Musalmán aristocracy was in defining their rights. Up to that period their title

[1] Mr. Westland's District of Jessor, p. 67. I refrain with difficulty from frequent reference to my Annals of Rural Bengal, and shall only add, that till arrangements are made for bringing the Bengal Records into intelligent contact with the European world, the Indian Government continues guilty of a great historical injustice to the British nation. But perhaps a Government which subverted a Power more extensive than that before which the majesty of Rome itself fell back, and which has built out of the shattered creeds and oppressed peoples of India a prosperous Empire, may be pardoned a noble indifference to the written memorials of its glory.

had not been permanent, but neither had it been fixed. At a costly sacrifice of the acknowledged claims of the ruling power, we gave them their tenures in perpetuity; but in doing so, we rendered these tenures inelastic. A race of men accustomed for centuries to the privilege of contemptuous plunder, could not, however, learn the peaceful art of managing their estates by the stroke of a Governor-General's pen. The Musalmán monopoly of rural oppression ceased, and the Resumption Laws thirty years later put a finishing stroke to their fortunes. To these laws I shall have to devote some paragraphs further on, and at present shall only say that they enriched the State by means of a stricter construction of title-deeds than the Muhammadans had ever been accustomed to under their own Emperors. During the last seventy-five years the Musalmán Houses of Bengal have either disappeared from the earth, or are at this moment being submerged beneath the new strata of society which our Rule has developed—haughty, insolent, indolent, but still the descendants of nobles and conquerors to the last.

With regard, therefore, to the first two great sources of Muhammadan wealth, viz. the Army and the higher administration of the Revenues, we had good reasons for what we did, but our action has brought ruin upon Muhammadan Houses of Bengal. We shut the Musalmán aristocracy out of the Army, because we believed that their exclusion was necessary to our own safety. We deprived them of their monopoly of the most lucrative functions in the Administration, because their deprivation was essential to the welfare and just government of the people. But these grounds, however good in themselves, fail to convince an ancient nobility suffering under the blight of British Rule. Their exclusion from the Army seems to the Musalmáns a great public wrong; our departure from their ancient fiscal system, an absolute breach of faith.

The third source of their greatness was their monopoly of Judicial, Political, or in brief, Civil Employ. It would be unfair to lay much stress on the circumstance, but it is nevertheless a significant fact, that none of the native gentlemen who have won their way into the Covenanted Civil Service, or up to the bench of the High Court, are Musalmáns. Yet for some time after the country passed under our care, the Musalmáns retained all the functions of Government in their own hands. Musalmán Collectors, as we have seen, gathered the Land-Tax; Musalmán *Faujdárs* and *Ghátwáls* officered the Police. A great Musalmán Department, with its headquarters in the Nizám's palace at Murshidabád, and a network of officials spreading over every District in the Province, administered the Criminal Law. Musalmán jailors took bribes from, or starved at their discretion, the whole prison population of Bengal. Kázis or Muhammadan Doctors of Law sat in the Civil and Domestic Courts. Even when we attempted to do justice by means of trained English officers, the Muhammadan Law Doctors sat with them as their authoritative advisers on points of law. The Code of Islám remained the law of the land, and the whole ministerial and subordinate offices of Government continued the property of the Musalmáns. They alone could speak the official language, and they alone could read the official records written in the Persian current hand.[1] The Cornwallis Code broke this monopoly less violently in the Judicial than in the Revenue departments; but for the first fifty years of the Company's Rule the Musalmáns

[1] *Shikastah*, literally broken, an abominable sort of shorthand with the vowels left out.

had the lion's share of State patronage. During its second half century of power the tide turned, at first slowly, but with a constantly accelerating pace, as the imperative duty of conducting public business in the vernacular of the people, and not in the foreign *patois* of its former Muhammadan conquerors, became recognised. Then the Hindus poured into, and have since completely filled, every grade of official life. Even in the District Collectorates of Lower Bengal, where it is still possible to give appointments in the old-fashioned friendly way, there are very few young Musalmán officials.[1] The Muhammadans who yet remain in them are white-bearded men, and they have no successors. Even ten years ago, the Musalmáns invariably managed to transmit the post of Názir, or Chief of the Revenue Bailiffs, to men of their own creed; but now one or two unpopular appointments about the jail are the most that the former masters of India can hope for. The staff of Clerks attached to the various offices, the responsible posts in the Courts, and even the higher offices in the Police, are recruited from the pushing Hindu youth of the Government School.[2]

Proceeding from the unconspicuous mass of non-gazetted officials to the higher grades, the question passes from the sphere of individual observation into the unquestionable domain of statistics. Two years ago I put forth a series of articles,[3] showing how completely the Judicial and Revenue Services in Bengal, in which the appointments are greatly coveted, and the distribution of patronage closely watched, had been denuded of Musalmáns. These

[1] Amlah.

[2] These remarks apply to the whole Province of Bengal, but with special force to every District of it, excepting those of the Bhagalpur and Patna Divisions.

[3] In the *Pioneer*, the leading journal of the North-West Provinces. I have freely used these articles in this Chapter.

articles were immediately translated into Persian, and copied into or discussed by many of the Anglo-Indian and vernacular papers. A Commission was issued by the Bengal Government to inquire into the higher class education of the Muhammadans in Calcutta; but the net result has been, that the Musalmán element in the public service has gone on growing weaker every year, just as before.

This statement the following statistics will prove. In the highest grade in which the appointments dated from a previous generation, the Muhammadans had not much to complain of, as in April 1869 there was one Musalmán to two Hindus: there is now but one Musalmán to three Hindus. In the second grade there were then two Muhammadans to nine Hindus; there is now one Musalmán to ten Hindus. In the third grade there were then four Musalmáns to a total of twenty-seven Hindus and Englishmen; there are now three Musalmáns to a total of twenty-four Hindus and Englishmen. Passing down to the lower ranks, there were in 1869 four Musalmáns among a total of thirty of all creeds; there are now four among a total of thirty-nine. Among the probationers from whom the service is recruited, there were only two Musalmáns in a total of twenty-eight; there is now not a single Muhammadan in this rank.

It is, however, in the less conspicuous Departments, in which the distribution of patronage is less keenly watched by the political parties in Bengal, that we may read the fate of the Musalmáns. In 1869 these Departments were filled thus:—In the three grades of Assistant Government Engineers there were fourteen Hindus and not one Musalmán; among the apprentices there were four Hindus and two Englishmen, and not one Musalmán. Among the sub-Engineers and Supervisors of the Public

Works Department there were twenty-four Hindus to one Musalmán; among the Overseers, two Musalmáns to sixty-three Hindus. In the Offices of Account there were fifty names of Hindus, and not one Musalmán; and in the Upper Subordinate Department there were twenty-two Hindus, and again not one Musalmán.

But it is unnecessary to multiply instances of a fact that is patent in every page of the Civil List. I have made up a table of the gazetted appointments for which Englishmen, Muhammadans, and Hindus are alike eligible:

DISTRIBUTION OF STATE PATRONAGE IN BENGAL, APRIL 1871.

| | Europeans. | Hindus. | Musalmáns. | TOTAL. |
|---|---|---|---|---|
| Covenanted Civil Service (appointed in England by the Crown), . . . . . . . | 260 | 0 | 0 | 260 |
| Judicial Officers in the Non-Regulation Districts,[1] | 47 | 0 | 0 | 47 |
| Extra Assistant Commissioners, . . . . . | 26 | 7 | 0 | 33 |
| Deputy-Magistrates and Deputy-Collectors, . . | 53 | 113 | 30 | 196 |
| Income-Tax Assessors, . . . . . . | 11 | 43 | 6 | 60 |
| Registration Department, . . . . . . | 33 | 25 | 2 | 60 |
| Judges of Small Cause Court and Subordinate Judges, . . . . . . . . . | 14 | 25 | 8 | 47 |
| Munsifs, . . . . . . . . . . . | 1 | 178 | 37 | 216 |
| Police Department, Gazetted Officers of all grades, | 106 | 3 | 0 | 109 |
| Public Works Department, Engineer Establishment, | 154 | 19 | 0 | 173 |
| ,, ,, Subordinate Establishment, | 72 | 125 | 4 | 201 |
| ,, ,, Account Establishment, . | 22 | 54 | 0 | 76 |
| Medical Department, Officers attached to Medical College, Jails, Charitable Dispensaries, Sanitation and Vaccination Establishments, and Medical Officers in charge of Districts, etc. etc., . | 89 | 65 | 4 | 158 |
| Department of Public Instruction, . . . . | 38 | 14 | 1 | 53 |
| Other Departments, such as Customs, Marine, Survey, Opium,[2] etc., . . . . . . | 412 | 10 | 0 | 422 |
| TOTAL, . | 1338 | 681 | 92 | 2111 |

[1] This and the following grades receive their appointments from the Local Government.

[2] But exclusive of the Ecclesiastical Establishment. Some of the Opium Officers are not gazetted.

A hundred years ago, the Musalmáns monopolized all the important offices of State. The Hindus accepted with thanks such crumbs as their former conquerors dropped from their table, and the English were represented by a few factors and clerks. The proportion of Muhammadans to Hindus, as shown above, is now less than one-seventh. The proportion of Hindus to Europeans is more than one-half; the proportion of Musalmáns to Europeans is less than one-fourteenth. The proportion of the race which a century ago had the monopoly of Government, has now fallen to less than one-twenty-third of the whole administrative body. This, too, in the gazetted appointments, where the distribution of patronage is closely watched. In the less conspicuous office establishments in the Presidency Town, the exclusion of Musalmáns is even more complete. In one extensive Department the other day it was discovered that there was not a single *employé* who could read the Musalmán dialect; and, in fact, there is now scarcely a Government office in Calcutta in which a Muhammadan can hope for any post above the rank of porter, messenger, filler of ink-pots, and mender of pens.

Is it that the Hindus have all along been better men than the Musalmáns, and only required a fair field in order to outstrip them in the race? Or is it that the Musalmáns have so many careers open to them in non-official life, that they are indifferent to Government employment, and leave the Hindus to walk over the course? The Hindu has unquestionably a high order of intellect; but an universal and immeasurable superiority on the part of the Hindus, such as would be required to explain their monopoly of official preferment, is unknown at the present day, and is in direct contradiction to their past history. The truth is, that when the country passed under our rule, the Musalmáns were the superior race, and superior not only in stoutness of heart and strength of arm, but in power of political organization, and in the science of practical government. Yet the Muhammadans are now shut out equally from Government employ and from the higher occupations of non-official life.

The only secular profession open to well-born Muhammadans is the Law. Medicine falls under a different category, as I shall afterwards show. Now the Law is even more strictly closed to the Muhammadans than the official services. Among the Judges of Her Majesty's High Court of Judicature in Bengal are two Hindus,[1] but no Musalmán. Indeed, the idea of a High Court Judge being taken from the race that once monopolized the whole administration of justice, is inconceivable alike to Anglo-Indians and to Hindus at the present day. In 1869, when I last made up the statistics of the Indian Professions, they stood thus:—The Law Officers of the Crown were six in number—four Englishmen, two Hindus, and no Musalmán. Among the Officers of the High Court of sufficient rank to have their names published, twenty-one in number, there were seven Hindu gentlemen, and not one Musalmán. Among the Barristers-at-Law were three Hindus (now greatly increased, I believe), and not one Musalmán.

But the list of Pleaders of the High Court, a sort of subordinate Barristers, tells the most cruel story of all. This was a branch of the Profession almost completely in the hands of the Musalmáns within the memory of men still living. The present list dates from 1834, and the surviving Pleaders of that year consisted in 1869 of one

[1] These gentlemen rank among the first grade of public servants; their salary is £5000 a year.

Englishman, one Hindu, and two Musalmáns. Up to 1838 the Musalmáns were almost as numerous as the Hindus and English put together, the proportion being six of the former to seven of both the latter. Of the Pleaders admitted between 1845 and 1850 inclusive, the whole survivors in 1869 were Musalmáns. Even as late as 1851 the Muhammadans stoutly held their own, and in fact equal the whole number of the English and Hindu Pleaders put together. From 1851 the scene changes. A new order of men began to come to the front. Different tests of fitness were exacted, and the list shows that out of two hundred and forty natives admitted from 1852 to 1868, two hundred and thirty-nine were Hindus, and only one a Musalmán.

Passing to the next grade in the Profession, the Attorneys, Proctors, and Solicitors of the High Court,[1] there were in 1869 twenty-seven Hindus and not one Musalmán; while among the rising generation of articled clerks there were twenty-six Hindus, and again not one Musalmán. It matters not to what department of the Profession I turn, the result is the same. In the Office of the Registrar of the High Court there were in 1869 seventeen *employés* of sufficient standing to have their names published. Six of them were Englishmen or East Indians, eleven were Hindus, and not one was a Musalmán. In the Receiver's Office four names were given, two Englishmen and two Hindus, but no Musalmán. In the Office of the Clerk of the Crown and Taxing Officer were four Englishmen and five Hindus, but no Musalmán. In all the nooks and crannies of the law, in the Offices of Account, the Sheriff's Office, Coroner's Office, and Office of Interpreters, twenty names were

[1] On the side of Original Jurisdiction.

given—eight Englishmen, eleven Hindus, and one Musalmán, the sole representative of the Muhammadan population on the list, and he a miserable *maula*[1] on six shillings a week.

The Profession of Medicine remains. But unhappily, Medicine, as practised by the native doctors, scarcely ranks as a Profession among the upper classes of Muhammadans. A Musalmán gentleman has two medical attendants. The one is a physician who, under the name of *Tabíb*, or, as he is generally designated by English writers, *Hakím*, receives honourable entertainment from his employers. The other is the *Jarráh*, which in simple English means barber. It is he who performs all surgical operations, from shaving to amputation; and so rigid is the line between Medicine and Surgery, that a *Tabíb* of good standing would refuse to bind up a wound. This line, however, the surgeon-barber by no means scruples to transgress. Practically, almost the whole science of Medicine falls within his jurisdiction, and the Muhammadan physicians proper are now a small and decaying class. In the great towns of Upper India they may still be found, but in the Bengal Districts they are never met with. The practice of Medicine has now fallen into the hands of the illiterate Musalmán barbers and of the Hindu doctors.[2]

Indeed, the traditional Muhammadan Physician, even where he still survives in Northern India, is a scholar and recluse rather than an active practitioner. He derives his art from Persian and Arabic manuscripts, and confounds our English science of Medicine with the despised occupation of the surgeon-barber. It thus happens that

1 Law-officer.

2 The Hindu doctors are also of two sorts: the *Kabiráj*, who practises on the native system of medicine, and is often a mere quack; and the trained medical man of our English Colleges.

in Bengal, where the State affords admirable facilities for the study of Medicine, the son of a good Musalmán family scarcely ever enters the Profession. Crowds of ill-bred Muhammadan boys from the lower and even the menial walks of life, jostle for just that amount of gratuitous instruction which will qualify them for a regimental apothecaryship. They are, in short, the barber-surgeons of a former time, despised by the upper classes of the Musalmán community, absolutely unrecognised by the few surviving Muhammadan physicians, thankless for the benefits which they receive, and insolent to their instructors except under the weight of an almost military discipline. It has been my good fortune to be intimately acquainted with many Hindu doctors whose bearing and whose learning entitle them to the respect due to their noble calling. But I have never met a single Musalmán doctor of this class. Such men may exist in Northern India, but in Bengal the Muhammadans do not seem to aspire to any of the recognised grades of the Medical Profession. In 1869 the statistics stood thus:—Among the Graduates of Medicine in the Calcutta University there were four doctors; three Hindus, one Englishman, and no Muhammadan. Among eleven Bachelors of Medicine, ten were Hindus and one an Englishman. The hundred and four Licentiates of Medicine consisted of five Englishmen, ninety-eight Hindus, and one solitary Muhammadan. Recently the Government conferred two titles of *Bahádur* upon members of the native medical profession immediately connected with the Calcutta University. Political considerations rendered it expedient that one of the titles should be given to a Hindu, the other to a Musalmán; and it is well known how highly the Muhammadans value such a distinction. Yet I hear that, notwithstanding the excellent personal qualities of the Musalmán gentleman selected, the title has failed to give him that social status among the higher classes of his countrymen which it generally confers. The truth is, that Muhammadans do not consider Medicine as taught in our schools the profession of a gentleman; and social prejudice closes this vocation to sons of good Muhammadan families, as completely as the other professions, and the Government Services are shut to them by the overpowering rush of highly-educated Hindus.

I have seldom read anything more piteous than the private letters and newspaper articles of Bengal Musalmáns. The Calcutta Persian paper[1] some time ago wrote thus:—'All sorts of employment, great and small, are being gradually snatched away from the Muhammadans, and bestowed on men of other races, particularly the Hindus. The Government is bound to look upon all classes of its subjects with an equal eye, yet the time has now come when it publicly singles out the Muhammadans in its Gazettes for exclusion from official posts. Recently, when several vacancies occurred in the office of the Sundarbans Commissioner, that official, in advertising them in the Government Gazette, stated that the appointments would be given to none but Hindus.[2] In short, the Muhammadans have now sunk so low, that, even when qualified for Government employ, they are studiously kept out of it by Government notifications. Nobody takes any notice of their helpless condition, and the higher authorities do not deign even to acknowledge their existence.'

[1] *Dúrbín*, of 14th July 1869.

[2] I have not at present the means of officially tracing and verifying this statement of the Persian journalist, but it attracted some notice at the time, and was not, so far as I heard, contradicted.

The following sentences are from a petition lately presented by the Orissa Muhammadans to the Commissioner.[1] Their stilted phraseology may perhaps raise a smile; but the permanent impression produced by the spectacle of the ancient conquerors of the Province begging in broken English for bare bread, is, I think, one of sorrowful silence:—'As loyal subjects of Her Most Gracious Majesty the Queen, we have, we believe, an equal claim to all appointments in the administration of the country. Truly speaking, the Orissa Muhammadans have been levelled down and down, with no hopes of rising again. Born of noble parentage, poor by profession, and destitute of patrons, we find ourselves in the position of a fish out of water. Such is the wretched state of the Muhammadans, which we bring unto your Honour's notice, believing your Honour to be the sole representative of Her Most Gracious Majesty the Queen for the Orissa Division, and hoping that justice will be administered to all classes, without distinction of colour or creed. The penniless and parsimonious condition which we are reduced to, consequent on the failure of our former Government service, has thrown us into such an everlasting despondency, that we speak from the very core of our hearts, that we would travel into the remotest corners of the earth, ascend the snowy peaks of the Himálaya, wander the forlorn regions of Siberia, could we be convinced that by so travelling we would be blessed with a Government appointment of ten shillings a week.'

How comes it that the Muhammadan population is thus shut out alike from official employ and from the recognised Professions? The Musalmáns of Bengal do not want intelligence, and the spur of poverty constantly

[1] Mr. E. W. Molony, C.S., to whom I am indebted for a copy.

goads them to do something to better their condition. The Government has covered Bengal with schools, and many of its Districts are peopled with Muhammadans; yet the Government schools fail to develop a class of Musalmáns who can compete successfully at the University, or find an entrance into any of the professions. The same schools send forth every year a vast body of well-read, ambitious, and intellectual Hindu youths, who distinguish themselves as young men at the University, and in after-life monopolize every avenue to wealth or distinction.

The truth is, that our system of public instruction, which has awakened the Hindus from the sleep of centuries, and quickened their inert masses with some of the noble impulses of a nation, is opposed to the traditions, unsuited to the requirements, and hateful to the religion, of the Musalmáns. Under Muhammadan Rule the Hindus accepted their fate exactly as they have done under our own. At present, preferment depends upon a knowledge of English, and they learn English. Formerly, preferment depended upon a knowledge of Persian, and they learned Persian. As far back as 1500 A.D. they had begun to compose works in that language. The verses of one of these early Hindu authors survive; and although an Infidel, he obtained a public position as a teacher of the Muhammadan youth, and a lecturer on their sciences. Under Akbar, the Hindus met the enlightened monarch half-way, and produced an eminent Persian poet. But it was not till a knowledge of Persian had become profitable to the Hindus that it became general among them. At the end of the sixteenth century the Chancellor of the Empire, himself a Hindu, commanded that the public accounts should thenceforward be written in Persian, and the Hindu subordinate Revenue Service forthwith learned Persian to a man. When, therefore, we introduced English into the public offices, the facile Hindu immediately mastered the language necessary to his success in life. The former language of public business under the Muhammadans, and the new one under ourselves, were alike foreign tongues to him. He was equally indifferent to both, except as a means of preferment; indeed, as our Government schools gave him this important talisman of success at less than half the cost price to the State, he greatly preferred our system to the one which had preceded it.

With the Musalmáns the case was altogether different. Before the country passed to us, they were not only the political but the intellectual power in India. 'They possessed a system of education which,' to use the words of the Indian statesman who knows them best, 'however inferior to that which we have established, was yet by no means to be despised; was capable of affording a high degree of intellectual training and polish; was founded on principles not wholly unsound, though presented in an antiquated form; and which was infinitely superior to any other system of education then existing in India;—a system which secured to them an intellectual as well as a material supremacy, and through the medium of which alone the Hindus could hope to fit themselves for the smallest share of authority in their native country.'[1] During the first seventy-five years of our Rule we continued to make use of this system as a means for producing officers to carry out our administration. But meanwhile we had introduced a scheme of Public Instruction of our own; and as soon as it trained

[1] Mr. E. C. Bayley, C.S.I.

up a generation of men on the new plan, we flung aside the old Muhammadan system, and the Musalmán youth found every avenue of public life closed in their faces.

Had the Musalmáns been wise, they would have perceived the change, and accepted their fate. But an ancient conquering race cannot easily divest itself of the traditions of its nobler days. The Bengal Muhammadans refused a system which gave them no advantages over the people whom they had so long ruled, a people whom they hated as idolaters and despised as a servile race. Religion came to the support of the popular feeling against the innovation, and for long it remained doubtful whether a Musalmán boy could attend our State Schools without perdition to his soul. Had we introduced our system by means of English masters, or boldly changed the language of public business to our own tongue, their religious difficulty would in one important respect have been less. For the Muhammadans admit that the Christian Faith, however short of the full truth as finally revealed by their Prophet, is nevertheless one of the inspired religions which have been vouchsafed to mankind. But Hinduism is to them the mystery of abominations, a system of devil-worship and idolatry unbroken by a single gleam of the knowledge of the One God.[1] The language of our Government Schools in Lower Bengal is Hindu, and the masters are Hindus. The higher sort of Musalmáns spurned the instructions of idolaters through the medium of the language of idolatry.

By degrees this detestation yielded to the altered necessities of the age. Religion, which had at the begin-

[1] I need hardly say that I totally disagree from this view, which is possibly still the view of some uninstructed Christians. The Muhammadans simply paid the price of their bigoted ignorance touching the faith of the people over whom they had so long ruled.

ning shed its sanction upon the popular dislike to our Schools, began to waver. Decisions by the most learned Law Doctor of the age, the Sun of India, who has already appeared more than once in this book, were wrested into an approval of an English education. This celebrated Professor had already decided as to employment under the English. Some official occupations, he had said, are desirable, others indifferent, and others sinful. Thus, if the English engage Musalmáns for praiseworthy posts, such as Law Officers according to the Muhammadan Code, overseers on roads or resting-houses for poor travellers, as protectors of property or suppressors of thieves, it is well. For thus 'the Prophet Joseph was employed as Treasurer and Inspector-General of Police to the Infidel King of Egypt, and likewise Her Highness Musí served Pharaoh for the purpose of suckling Moses.' But if the service tends to make a person irreligious, then the Musalmán who accepts it commits sin.

In the same way, when his disciples asked him whether it was lawful to learn logic or English, he replied:—'Logic is not necessary for salvation, but it is a help like grammar in learning the necessary knowledge. If any man learns it in order to cast doubts on religion, he is a sinner. But if he learns it for learning's sake, he is guiltless. Learning English for the purpose of reading books, writing letters, and knowing the secret meanings of words, is permitted; because Zeid Ibn Sábit learned the language and dictionaries of the Jews and Christians by the Prophet's order, that he might be able to answer the letters which the Jews and Christians sent to the Prophet. But if any man learns English for pleasure, or in order to unite himself with the English, he sins and transgresses the Law: even as in the case of a weapon of iron, if the weapon is made for driving away thieves or for arresting them, then the making of it is a pious act; but if it is made to help or defend the thieves, then the making of it is sinful.'

The more zealous Muhammadans, however, have never quite accepted the lawfulness of an education in our State Schools. While the worldly-minded among them made advances towards our system, the fanatical section shrunk still further back from it. During the last forty years they have separated themselves from the Hindus by differences of dress, of salutations, and other exterior distinctions, such as they never deemed necessary in the days of their supremacy. Even as late as 1860–62 there was only one Musalmán to ten Hindus in our schools; and although the proportion has increased since then, the increase is due to the additional Aided Institutions, and not to the District Government Schools. The attendance at the English Schools has not increased; and the officer in charge of the Wahábi prosecutions, on whose authority I make these statements, and who is intimately acquainted with Eastern Bengal, declares that the number of Muhammadan students bears no fair ratio to the Muhammadan population.

The truth is, that our system of Public Instruction ignores the three most powerful instincts of the Musalmán heart. In the first place, it conducts education in the vernacular of Bengal, a language which the educated Muhammadans despise, and by means of Hindu teachers, whom the whole Muhammadan community hates. The Bengáli schoolmaster talks his own dialect and a vile Urdu, the latter of which is to him an acquired language almost as much as it is to ourselves. Moreover, his gentle and timid character unfits him to maintain order among

Musalmán boys. 'Nothing on earth,' said a Muhammadan husbandman recently to an English official, 'would induce me to send my boy to a Bengáli teacher.' In the second place, our rural schools seldom enable a Muhammadan to learn the tongues necessary for his holding a respectable position in life, and for the performance of his religious duties. Every Muhammadan gentleman must have some knowledge of Persian, and Persian is a language unknown even in our higher class District schools. Every Musalmán, from the peasant to the prince, ought to say his prayers in one of the sacred languages, Persian[1] or Arabic, and this our schools have never recognised. It was lately asserted on high authority, that the prayers of the Musalmáns find no acceptance with God unless they are offered in the prescribed tongues. In the third place, our system of Public Instruction makes no provision for the religious education of the Muhammadan youth. It overlooks the fact that among the Hindus a large and powerful caste has come down from time immemorial for supplying this part of a boy's training, while among the Muhammadans no separate body of clergy exists. Every head of a Musalmán household is supposed to know the duties of his religion, and to be his own family priest. Public ministrations are indeed conducted at the mosques; but it is the glory of Islám that its temples are not made with hands, and that its ceremonies can be performed anywhere upon God's earth or under His heavens. A system of purely secular education is adapted to very few nations. In the opinion of many deeply thinking men, it has signally failed in Ireland, and it is certainly altogether unsuited to the illiterate and fanatical peasantry of Muhammadan Bengal.

[1] Persian has become a quasi-sacred language with the Bengáli Musalmáns, as it was the vehicle through which the Law and the Scriptures of Islám reached them.

'Is it therefore,' to repeat the words of the Indian Statesman who has studied the subject most deeply, 'any wonder that the Musalmáns have held aloof from a system which made no concession to their prejudices; made no provision for what they esteemed their necessities; which was in its nature unavoidably antagonistic to their interests, and at variance with all their social traditions?'

Yet many English Officers have gone through their service with a chronic indignation against the Muhammadans for refusing to accept the education which we have tried to bring to every man's door. The facility with which the rest of the population acquiesced in it made this refusal more odious by contrast. The pliant Hindu knew no scruples, and we could not understand why the Muhammadan should be troubled with them. But the truth is, that we overlooked a distinction as old as the religious instinct itself,—the distinction which in all ages and among all nations has separated polytheism from the worship of One God. Polytheism, by multiplying the objects of its followers' adoration, divides its claims on their belief. What Gibbon finely said of the Greeks, applies at this moment with more than its original force to the Hindus: 'Instead of an indivisible and regular system which occupies the whole extent of the believing mind, the mythology of the Greeks was composed of a thousand loose and flexible parts, and the servant of the gods was at liberty to define the degree and measure of his religious faith.'[1] The Muhammadans have no such licence. Their creed demands an absolute, a living, and even an intolerant belief; nor will any system of Public Instruction, which leaves the religious principle out of sight, ever satisfy the devout follower of Islám.

[1] Roman Empire, vol. ii. p. 360, quarto ed. of 1786.

How far it may be possible to do justice to the Musalmán population in this respect, without sacrificing our position as a Christian Government, I shall afterwards inquire. Meanwhile the Muhammadans have just ground for complaining that the funds which we levy impartially from all classes for State Education, are in Bengal expended on a system exclusively adapted to the Hindus.

But unfortunately this is not their most serious charge against us. While we have created a system of Public Instruction unsuited to their wants, we have also denuded their own system of the funds by which it was formerly supported. Every great Musalmán House in Bengal maintained a scholastic establishment in which its sons and its poorer neighbours received an education free of expense. As the Muhammadan families of the Province declined, such private institutions dwindled in numbers and in efficiency. It was not, however, till the second half century of our Rule that we arrayed against them the resistless force of British Law. From time immemorial the Native Princes of India had been accustomed to set apart grants of land for the education of the youth and for the service of the gods. The ruling power for the time being always possessed unquestioned and unlimited powers in this respect. Under the careless sway of the Mughuls, and during the anarchy amid which their Empire closed, the power had been to some extent transferred to, and to a still greater extent usurped by, the Provincial Governors and their subordinates. The distant Dehli Court troubled itself little about what was going on in Lower Bengal, so long as the total tribute of the Province was discharged. The indolent and luxurious Governor at Dacca or Murshidabád was equally indifferent to the details of the District Administration.

Every great Farmer of the Revenue could do pretty much as he liked with the lands under his care, so long as he paid up the stipulated Land-Tax. According to the form of his religion, he gave rent-free tenures to the temples or to the mosques, and a long life of cruelty and extortion might always be condoned by liberal death-bed devises *in pios usus.*

When we took over charge of Bengal, the ablest Revenue Officer of the time[1] estimated that one-fourth of the whole Province had been transferred from the State. In 1772 Warren Hastings discerned the gigantic fraud, but the feeling against resuming such tenures was then too strong to allow of any active steps being taken. In 1793 Lord Cornwallis again asserted in the strongest and broadest manner the inalienable right of Government to all rent-free grants which had not obtained the sanction of the Ruling Power. But even the powerful Government of that day did not venture to carry out this principle. The subject rested for another quarter of a century, until 1819, when the Government again asserted its rights, but again shrank from enforcing them. It was not until 1828 that the Legislature and the Executive combined to make one great effort. Special Courts were created, and during the next eighteen years the whole Province was overrun with informers, false witnesses, and stern pale-faced Resumption Officers.

At an outlay of £800,000 upon Resumption proceedings, an additional revenue of £300,000 a year was permanently gained by the State, representing a capital at five per cent. of six millions sterling.[2] A large part of

[1] Mr. James Grant.

[2] Vide *Friend of India* of 30th April 1846, whose calculations have been accepted by subsequent Revenue Authorities; *e.d.* Mr. J. H. Young, C. S., in the Revenue Handbook, p. 69. Calcutta, 1861.

this sum was derived from lands held rent free by Musalmáns or by Muhammadan foundations. The panic and hatred which ensued have stamped themselves for ever on the rural records. Hundreds of ancient families were ruined, and the educational system of the Musalmáns, which was almost entirely maintained by rent-free grants, received its death-blow. The scholastic classes of the Muhammadans emerged from the eighteen years[1] of harrying, absolutely ruined. Any impartial student will arrive at the conviction, that while the Resumption Laws only enforced rights which we had again and again most emphatically reserved, yet that the Resumption Proceedings were harsh in the extreme, and opposed to the general sense of the Indian people. Prescription cannot create rights in the face of express enactments, but seventy-five years of unbroken possession give rise to strong claims on the tenderness of a Government. Our Resumption Officers knew no pity. They calmly enforced the law. The panic of those days is still remembered, and it has left to us a bitter legacy of hatred. Since then the profession of a Man of Learning, a dignified and lucrative calling under Native Rulers, has ceased to exist in Bengal.

The Muhammadan foundations suffered most; for with regard to their title-deeds, as with regard to all other matters, the former conquerors of India had displayed a haughty indifference unknown to the provident and astute Hindu. We demanded an amount of proof in support of rent-free tenures, which, in the then uncertain state of real-property law, they could not have pro-

[1] The Resumption proceedings were fiercest at the beginning, and after languishing for some years, were officially terminated by the Government Order of March 4, 1846.

duced in support of their acknowledged private estates. During seventy-five years we had submitted under protest to a gigantic system of fraud, and the accumulated penalty fell upon a single generation. Meanwhile the climate and the white-ants had been making havoc of the grants and title-deeds which might have supported their claims. There can be little doubt that our Resumptions fell short of what had been stolen from us; but there can be no doubt whatever, that from those Resumptions the decay of the Muhammadan system of education dates. The officer now in charge of the Wahábi prosecutions cites them as the second cause of the decline of the Musalmán community in Bengal.

The justice of these proceedings may, however, be defended; the absolute misappropriation of scholastic funds, with which the Musalmáns charge us, cannot. For it is no use concealing the fact that the Muhammadans believe that, if we had only honestly applied the property entrusted to us for that purpose, they would at this moment possess one of the noblest and most efficient educational establishments in Bengal. In 1806 a wealthy Muhammadan gentleman of Hugli District died, leaving a vast estate *in pios usus.* Presently his two trustees began to quarrel. In 1810 the dispute deepened into a charge of malversation, and the English Collector of the District attached the property, pending the decision of the Courts. Litigation continued till 1816, when the Government dismissed both the trustees, and assumed the management of the estate, appointing itself in the place of one trustee, and nominating a second one. Next year it let out the estate in perpetuity, taking a suitable payment from each of the permanent lease-holders. These payments, with the arrears which had accumulated during the litigation, now amount to £105,700,[1] besides over £12,000 which has since been saved from the annual proceeds of the estate.

The Trust had, as I have said, been left for pious uses. These uses had been defined by the will, such as the maintenance of certain religious rites and ceremonies, the repair of the *Imámbárah* or great mosque at Hugli, a burial ground, certain pensions, and various religious establishments. An educational foundation came strictly within the purposes of the Trust, but an educational establishment on the Muhammadan plan, such as the founder would have himself approved. A College for poor scholars has always been considered 'a pious use' in Musalmán countries. But any attempt to divert the funds to a non-Muhammadan College would have been deemed an act of impiety by the testator, and could only be regarded as a gross malversation on the part of the trustees. Indeed, so inseparable is the religious element from a Muhammadan endowment, that the Government had to carefully investigate the legality of applying a Trust, made by a gentleman of the Shiah sect, to the education of the Sunni Musalmáns.

We may imagine, then, the burst of indignation with which the Muhammadans learned that the English Government was about to misappropriate the funds to the erection of an English College. This, however, it did. It devoted an estate left expressly for the pious uses of Islám, to founding an institution subversive in its very nature of the principles of Islám, and from which the Muhammadans were practically excluded. At this moment the head of the College is an English gentleman ignorant of a single word of Persian or Arabic, who draws

[1] The College building, however, was paid for out of this source.

£1500 a year from a Muhammadan religious endowment for teaching things hateful to every Musalmán. It is not, of course, his fault, but the fault of the Government which placed him there, and which for thirty-five years has been deliberately misappropriating this great educational fund. In vain it attempted to cloak so gross a breach of trust by attaching a small Muhammadan school to the English College. Besides the misappropriation of the accumulated fund in building the College, it annually diverted £5000 to its maintenance. That is to say, out of an income of £5260, it devoted only £350 to the little Muhammadan school which alone remained to bear witness to the original character of the Trust.

It is painful to dwell on this charge of misappropriation, because it is impossible to rebut it. The Muhammadans declare that the English took advantage of irregularities on the part of the first Musalmán trustees, to place an Infidel Government in charge of their largest religious endowments; and that they have since aggravated this initial wrong by substituting for the 'pious objects' of the Musalmán testator, an Institution which is of no service to the Muhammadans whatever. Some years ago it is stated that, out of three hundred boys in the English College, not one per cent. were Musalmáns; and although this disgraceful disproportion has since been lessened, the sense of injustice still remains among the Muhammadan community. 'I believe it is difficult,' writes a Civilian who has studied the matter deeply, 'to over-estimate the odium, not to say the contempt, which the British Government has incurred by its action in this case. This language may perhaps be deemed strong, but I can testify to the fact that during twenty-eight years' residence in India I have repeatedly broached the subject (I visited Hugli within a few weeks after my first arrival), and I can affirm that I never heard from native or European any other account. Rightly or not, the Muhammadans *do* think that Government has behaved unjustly, and even meanly, towards them in this matter, and it is a standing sore and grievance with them.'

Even this, however, does not complete the wrongs with which the Musalmáns charge their English Rulers. They arraign us not only upon depriving them of any chance of success in this life, but also upon attempts to imperil their salvation in the next. All religions of the noble type have set apart certain days for the performance of their spiritual duties. We can picture the sorrow and indignation with which the English would regard the arbitrary fiat of a foreign conqueror, declaring that Sundays should no longer be days of rest. The Muhammadans venerate with emotions of equal tenderness their own solemn festivals. In most parts of India we have respected this feeling. But in Lower Bengal the Muhammadans have of late so completely sunk out of sight, that their religious requirements were gradually overlooked, then neglected, and finally denied. Last year the Muhammadan Pleaders of the High Court presented two memorials on this subject. They pointed out, that while the number of closed days allowed to the Christians were sixty-two in number, and those to the Hindus fifty-two, only eleven were granted to the Muhammadans. Formerly the sanctioned Musalmán holidays amounted to twenty-one; and all that the petitioners ventured to beg was, that they should not be further decreased below the minimum of eleven which they had already reached. These memorials were called forth by an order that the native holidays observed by the High Court should hereafter be the same as those allowed in other Government Offices. Now, 'in other Government Offices' no Muhammadan holidays are sanctioned at all. The head of each establishment may allow any Muhammadans whom he may have under him to absent themselves during their six great fasts or festivals, making a total of twelve days per annum; but the office remains open, and the general work goes on as usual.

The Muhammadan Pleaders pointed out that a permissive system of this sort would by no means meet the requirements of a public Court of Justice. Such tribunals have to consider not only their officers and practitioners, but also the public for whose convenience they exist. They urged that, although the number of Muhammadan Pleaders has greatly diminished, yet that the number of Muhammadan suitors who come to look after their cases has, in consequence of railway communication, more than proportionately increased. That even if the Muhammadan Pleaders might be excused from attendance on a Muhammadan holiday, yet that they could not divert their minds from suits which might still be carried on if a Hindu or an English Pleader happened to be also engaged in them. In short, that the order amounted to a total abolition of their religious festivals,—an abolition opposed to the practice of the seventy-two years during which the Court had sat, and prohibitive of the duties enjoined by their faith. 'If holidays are to be allowed to Hindus and Christians according to their religion, your Memorialists submit that the Muhammadans should not be deprived of the holidays set apart for the performance of their religious duties and ceremonies.'[1] The hardship is aggra-

[1] Memorial of the Muhammadan Pleaders of the High Court to the Officiating Chief-Justice and his companion Justices, para. 3.

vated by the fact that, with the exception of two festivals (the *'Id-ul-fitr* occupying three days, and the *'Id-uz-zuhá* occupying one), all the Musalmán holidays are seasons of humiliation and mourning, during which every religious man should shut out the affairs of the world and take account with his soul.

To so low an estate has the race which once monopolized the whole legal appointments throughout India fallen in Bengal. It is gratifying to know that at least this piece of injustice was not allowed to take effect. The Supreme Government interfered and authoritatively set apart a certain limited number of Muhammadan holidays; not, indeed, so many as the Musalmáns desired, but as many as the exigencies of public business would permit, and sufficient for the observance of the great festivals of their faith.

One charge yet remains. The Muhammadans complain that not only has our system extruded them from the legal profession, but that an Act of the Legislature has deprived them of the one essential functionary for the fulfilment of their domestic and religious law. Under a Muhammadan Government, the Kázi unites many of the functions of a criminal, a civil, and an ecclesiastical judge. It was to him that we chiefly trusted to carry on the administration of justice when we first took charge of the country. Our earliest code recognised his importance and confirmed his office, and a long list of twenty-five Regulations touching his duties may still be found in our Indian Statute Books.[1] Indeed, so in-

[1] BENGAL CODE.—Reg. IV., 1793; Reg. XII., 1793; Reg. XXXIX., 1793; Reg. VIII., 1795; Reg. XI., 1795; Reg. XLIX., 1795; Reg. II., 1798; Reg. III., 1803; Reg. XI., 1803; Reg. XLVI., 1803; Reg. X., 1806; Reg. VIII., 1809; Reg. XVIII., 1817; Reg. XI., 1826; Reg. III., 1827; Reg. III., 1829. MADRAS CODE.—Reg. XI., 1802; Reg. III., 1808; Reg. VII., 1822; Reg. III., 1828.

dispensable is the Kázi to the Muhammadan domestic and religious code, that the law-doctors decided that India would continue a Country of Islám so long as the Kázis were maintained, and become a Country of the Enemy the moment they were abolished.

Unfortunately, the intimate acquaintance with Muhammadan popular feeling, which Muhammadan disaffection has now forced us to acquire, is of a very recent date. In 1863, one of the Provincial Governors called in question the propriety of continuing to appoint Kázis. He appears to have thought that such appointments involved a recognition of their sacerdotal character by the Government, and to have believed that the Muhammadan community might be safely allowed to make the appointments themselves. Accordingly, after some discussion, and a strong protest from Bombay, the whole previous legislation on the subject was repealed, and Government formally discontinued its appointment of Kázis.[1]

During the past seven years a great and constantly increasing section of the Muhammadan community have been deprived of the functionary necessary for the celebration of marriages and other important ceremonies of their domestic Code. The evil did not tell at first so severely as afterwards, for the old Kázis remained. It was only on the death or retirement of one of them that the law took effect, by having abolished the machinery for filling his place. The subject early attracted the attention of the present Viceroy, but no absolutely con-

BOMBAY CODE.—Reg. II., 1827; and Reg. XXVI., 1827. Act XXVII. of 1836; Act VII. of 1843; and Act V. of 1845.

[1] By Act XI. of 1864, subsequently repealed by the schedule attached to Act VIII. of 1868, which, however, did not revive the old Regulations under which the appointments had formerly been made.

clusive evidence could be obtained until in 1870 the Madras High Court took up and decided the question. Mr. Justice Collett's decision[1] leaves no doubt that Kázis can only be appointed by the ruling Power; that in default of such appointment the Muhammadans are powerless to elect one themselves; and that the Act of 1864 has deprived their community of the most important officer of their law. His duties are defined as preparing and attesting Deeds of Transfer, celebrating marriages, and performing certain other religious rites and ceremonies. Now it so happens that one of the crying evils in Lower Bengal which embarrasses and defies the Magistrates is marriage litigation among the Muhammadans. For some reason or another, the marriage tie has of late been relaxed. Charges of adultery or abduction, both of which come under the Penal Code, pour into the Courts of the Deltaic Districts, and in nine cases out of ten it is impossible to prove the legality of the marriage. Such cases in the two Divisions of Eastern Bengal rose from 561 in 1862, two years before the discontinuance of the official appointment of Kázis, to 1984 in 1866, or two years after that discontinuance. Since then the number has decreased in the Criminal Returns, apparently not from any real diminution, but because it has become customary to refer such complaints to the Civil Courts.[2]

I take these figures from a valuable note by the officer in charge of the Wahábi prosecutions, and an

[1] Original Suit, No. 453 of 1869; Muhammad Abubakr *v.* Mir Ghulám Husain and Another.

[2] The excessive growth of marriage litigation was to some extent due to the people learning more fully how to make use of the Indian Penal Code. But the fact of our having rendered breaches of the marriage tie a criminal offence made it the more important that the marriage law should be well defined. We took the very worst moment that could possibly have been chosen for the abolition of the Musalmán marriage officers.

official of still greater weight and experience thus sums up the political evil that the discontinuance of officially appointing Kázis has done:—'In connection with the Wahábi movement, there is, I think, no doubt that their abolition has acted in two ways. It has increased the number of zealous partially instructed men of letters,[1] who, without other means of livelihood, and embittered against the existing state of things, go about preaching among the ignorant Muhammadan population, apostles of disloyalty. But it also acts in a far more serious way. There can be no doubt that a Muhammadan's life can hardly be conducted in conformity to the rules of his religion where no proper Kázi exists. Not only do certain ceremonies require their sanction, but there are perpetually small questions of religious and formal law cropping up in the every-day life of a Muhammadan, which should properly be resolved by a Kázi. If no such officer exists, it gives a broad opening to a man who is disloyal to Government to press on a conscientious Muhammadan that the Government is not one he can properly live under. On the other hand, the use and recognition of a Kázi appointed by Government is virtually a recognition of the authority and lawfulness of that Government.'

The question is one of the most important that ever came before the Indian Legislature. Under an acknowledged military occupation, as in Algiers, it may be doubtful how far the Kázis require recognition by the Ruling Power. But all the evidence tends to show that such recognition or appointment *is* necessary under a settled Civil Government like that of British India. The point

[1] The class from whom the Kázis were recruited, and who looked to that office as their career in life.

is an intricate one, but meanwhile the decision of the Madras High Court remains in force, and leaves the office of Kázi shorn of dignity and legal authority. Deep consideration of the whole bearings of the case, and consultation with the ten Provincial Governments into which India is divided, will no doubt be required before a decision can be safely arrived at. But the earnest attitude which the Viceroy has taken up, and the firm resolve of Government to do justice to the Muhammadans, at whatever cost of admitting its former mistakes, give good ground for belief that this too will presently be removed from the list of Musalmán charges against British Rule.

The neglect and contempt with which, for half a century, the Muhammadan population of Lower Bengal has thus been treated, have left their marks deep in recent Indian literature. The former conquerors of the East are excluded from our Oriental journals and libraries as well as from the more active careers in life. The old Court of Directors wisely shared its favours between Musalmáns and Hindus, and the admirable Arabic and Persian scholarship displayed in the earlier series of the Bibliotheca Indica was merely the literary representative of this political impartiality. But during the last fifty years the Hindus have extruded the Muhammadans alike from State literature and State employ, and the £600 a year which the Court of Directors granted to the Bibliotheca Indica has been allotted in almost as one-sided a way as Bengal official patronage. Between 1847 and 1852, under Dr. Roer's rule, few efforts of Semitic scholarship appeared; and although, during the brief incumbency of Dr. Sprenger, a reaction set in, and two works of the first magnitude were begun, they have been left unfinished.

Dr. Horace Hayman Wilson's enthusiastic Sanskrit scholarship could ill brook the expenditure of an Indian grant upon Arabic literature. Under his inspiration, the Court of Directors issued an injunction that the Bibliotheca Indica should be devoted entirely to Indian subjects, upon pain of withdrawal of the £600 a year. Perhaps it was well that a man with so much force of character, and with such paramount claims to be heard on his own subject, should have been temporarily allowed to have his way. Dr. H. H. Wilson built the basement of modern Sanskrit learning; the masonry which Max Müller is now overlaying with his exquisite ornamentation, and upon which he is rearing upper storeys of a light and graceful architecture hitherto unattempted in scholarship. Meanwhile Goldstücker, Aufrecht, Fitz-Edward Hall, and Muir are strengthening the foundation, throwing out buttresses, and adding substantial wings, so that the beautiful structure shall abide for ever.

But a little band of Semitic scholars were still holding together, and defending their position to the last. The Court of Directors had withdrawn its support from any undertaking extraneous to India Proper. The Semitic scholars did not feel strong enough to fight on this ground, and accordingly abandoned the Arabic outworks; only to entrench themselves, however, behind the Persian literature of the Muhammadan Empire. Sir Henry Elliot went on with his labours unmoved. Mr. Thomas, Mr. Hammond, Sir William Muir, and a few others, formed a brilliant group of Civilians, who wrung from the Local Government what the distant Court of Directors had refused. In 1855 the Lieutenant-Governor of the North-West Provinces sanctioned the collection of Persian MSS. at the public expense. Sixty-seven were landed at a single haul. The publication of Sir Henry Elliot's papers, under the admirable although somewhat leisurely editorship of Mr. Thomas, Professor Dowson, and Mr. Beames, marks a vast stride. Meanwhile the Lucknow Muhammadan Presses have been annually pouring forth their varied, if not very careful or well-considered, productions. Colonel Nassau Lees has devoted all his influence and learning to the cause; and in Dr. Rost, the new librarian at the India Office, Orientalists have obtained one of those rare scholars who combine a broad range of subjects and interests with depth and absolute trustworthiness. In India the reaction is equally well marked, and a scholar has arisen in the person of Mr. Blochmann, whose industry, talent, and enthusiasm recall the early days of Oriental learning.

I have now set forth the Muhammadan Petition and Complaint against British Rule. The charges of misappropriation and specific wrongs may be safely left to Government to deal with,—a Government which has during the last two years shown its earnestness equally in putting down disaffection and in trying to remove the causes of it. But on the more general and less tangible accusation of neglect I must say a few words. If we analyse this charge, we shall find that our unsympathetic system of Public Instruction lies at the root of the matter. The Bengal Musalmáns can never hope to succeed in life, or to obtain a fair share of the State patronage, until they fit themselves for it, and they will never thus fit themselves until provision is made for their education in our schools. The changes required are, in my opinion, very simple and inexpensive. But before entering on them, I propose to relate the one great effort we have made in this direction. The English in India have failed in their duty towards the Musalmáns, but it is only fair to narrate the difficulties and discouragements which they have met with in trying to do it.

During exactly ninety years, a costly Muhammadan College has been maintained in Calcutta at the State expense.[1] It owes its origin, like most other of the English attempts to benefit the people, to Warren Hastings. In 1781 the Governor-General discerned the change which must inevitably come over the prospects of the Musalmáns, and tried to prepare them for it. As the wealth of the great Muhammadan Houses decayed, their power of giving their sons an education which should fit them for the higher offices in the State declined *pari passu*. To restore the chances in their favour, Warren Hastings established a Muhammadan College in the Capital, and 'endowed it with certain rents towards its perpetual maintenance.' Unfortunately for the Musalmáns, he left its management to the Musalmáns themselves. Persian and Arabic remained the sole subjects of instruction, long after Persian and Arabic had ceased to be the bread-winners in official life. Abuses of a very grave character crept into the College, and in 1819 it was found necessary to appoint an European Secretary. In 1826 a further effort was made to adapt the Institution to the altered necessities of the times; an English class was formed, but unhappily soon afterwards broken up. Three years afterwards, another and a more permanent effort was made, but with inadequate results. During the next quarter of a century, the Muhammadan College shared the fate of the Muhammadan community. It was allowed to drop out of sight; and when the Local Government made any sign on the subject, it was some

[1] Known in Bengal as the *Madraseh.*

expression of impatience at its continuing to exist at all.

Between 1851 and 1853, however, the authorities awoke to the necessity of doing something towards reforming an Institution which had become a public scandal. The result of the proposals then put forward[1] amounted to this. The College was divided into two Departments, the lower of which, under the name of the Anglo-Persian Branch, taught Urdu, Persian, and English up to a very moderate standard.[2] The upper Department was devoted entirely to Arabic. The defects of this plan soon became apparent. When the youths passed into the purely Arabic Branch, they forgot what they had learned in the more miscellaneous lower Department. In 1858 the effects of the system are thus described: 'It turned out a few scholars, good in their peculiar narrow way, but not in the least fitted to take their place in the competition of official or general life; and who were in consequence, as a class, bigoted, self-sufficient, disappointed, and soured, if not disloyal.'[3]

Another effort was made to reform the College, and for a year or two with some success.[4] But things soon relapsed into their former state, and in 1869 the Bengal Government had to issue a Commission, still sitting, to

[1] By Mr. J. R. Colvin, the Civilian who then chiefly enjoyed the confidence of the Muhammadan community, as from his accomplishments in Persian and Arabic he deserved it, and who, on the death of Mr. Thomason, became Lieutenant-Governor of the North-Western Provinces. He died in the Agra Fort during the Mutiny.

[2] At present, to the entrance standard of the Calcutta University.

[3] Mr. E. C. Bayley, to whose notes I owe several of the ideas contained in this Chapter.

[4] Under the suggestion of Colonel Nassau Lees, the Honorary Principal of the College. It is only fair to Colonel Lees (who is not now in India to speak for himself), to state that he again and again earnestly set forth the necessity for reform, and that some of the proposals which I shall make later on were urged by him many years ago.

inquire into the causes of its inefficiency. The truth is, that the Muhammadan College fitted its students neither for the University nor for active life. 'The whole system,' says the most distinguished Musalmán Reformer of the day,[1] 'can land them only in half-and-half results. As students entirely of Arabic, they lose the benefit of the little English training they were acquainted with; for the College has no means for continuing English instruction, and it does not take much time to obliterate from their minds whatever little English they may have learned.'

I propose briefly to explain how so sad a result has been obtained from so well-meant an effort. In the first place, the supervision has been all along deficient. Even during the brief period that an English Principal has existed, his appointment and his authority have been little more than nominal. He has had charge of other and more important offices; and to these the Principalship of the one great Muhammadan College which we have in Bengal has been tacked on as a sort of honorary appointment, with a merely nominal addition to his other salary. For example, the present Principal's chief appointment is Secretary to the Board of Examiners; and through his hands the whole of the Military Officers at the Presidency have to pass, in order to qualify themselves for appointments, with all the Civilians who read for honours in the native languages. He is also officiating as Assistant-Secretary and Translator to the Government of India in the Home Department, besides any occasional work which may be thrown upon him, such as Committees and miscellaneous references from Government. In addition to all this, he is supposed to be Principal of the Muhammadan College; and however enthusiastically the

[1] Maulaví Abd-ul-Latíf Khán Bahádur.

present incumbent may have entered on this fragment of his multifarious duties, it is hopeless to look for permanent efficiency from such a system.

The internal arrangements are still worse. An able and energetic scholar presides over the lower Department, but his control ends just where such supervision is most needed, viz. in the higher Arabic Branch. This Department, on which the whole success of the Institution depends, is left in the hands of the native Maulavís. Nominally, indeed, one of the latter gentlemen enjoys precedence over the other Masters, with the title of Head Maulaví. But no distinct chain of subordination exists; the under Masters were not responsible to him, and he was never seen out of his own class.[1] There were no monthly nor quarterly examinations; no daily, nor even weekly, inspections of the classes. It is clear that no good could come out of such a system. The Principal could not really superintend, because he had other work; the Head Maulaví never attempted to supervise, and we know the practical results.

It is impossible to exaggerate the evil which this neglect has done to the Muhammadan youth of Bengal. We must remember that, since we misappropriated the Hugli Endowment a generation ago, the Calcutta College is the one Institution where they can hope to obtain a high-class education. A body of young Musalmáns, about a hundred in number, are gathered together in the heart of a licentious Oriental capital; kept under bad influences for seven years, with no check upon their conduct, and no examples of honourable efficiency within their sphere;

[1] I do not know whether the fact of a Commission being actually sitting has changed matters in this and the other respects subsequently mentioned. But I guarantee the absolute accuracy of my statements as representing the general conduct of the College when the Commission was appointed.

and finally sent back to their native villages without being qualified for any career in life. About eighty per cent. of them come from the fanatical Eastern Districts;[1] the difficulty of getting any lucrative employment, without a knowledge of English, having driven away the youth of the more loyal parts of Bengal from the College. The students have passed their boyhood in an atmosphere of disaffection. Many of them are poor, and when they come to Calcutta, lodge in the houses and live on the charity of English gentlemen's butlers.[2] These are the moneyed men among the Muhammadan community, and they deride their masters behind their backs with all the suppressed insolence of menials belonging to a subject race. The students are all above sixteen, some above twenty, and some, I am told, over thirty years of age. The butlers with whom they live not only acquire the religious merit of supporting them, but often marry their daughters, with a handsome dowry, to their guests. The latter come from the petty landholding class, who care nothing for English or for science, little for Persian, and a great deal for the technicalities of Arabic grammar and law. At home they were engaged in ploughing their little fields or plying their boats; and they speak the rude peasant dialect of the Deltaic Districts—a *patois* unintelligible to the Calcutta Musalmán.

This is the new-caught student. In a few years he loses his barbarous jargon, gets his beard clipped, and sets up as a young professor of the Musalmán Law. A generous Government allows twenty-eight scholarships among the hundred students, so that sooner or later any

[1] Chittagong, Sandwíp, and Sháhbázpúr send the majority.

[2] Khánsámáns, who maintain poor scholars as a religious act. Such board and lodging is called a *jágír*, the name by which the military fiefs of the Muhammadan Empire were styled.

youth of the smallest application is sure to get one. Meanwhile the more enterprising and less studious among them set up a little trade. The advanced student has a consequential swagger all his own. He struts about Calcutta with his books under his arm, and, throwing aside the character of a poor pensioner, demands the respect due to a man of learning from the butler on whom he lives. Thanks to our short-sighted abolition of the Kázis, the domestic Code of Islám has fallen into the hands of unlicensed practitioners. The College Students read the marriage formula in the lower sort of Muhammadan families, settle matters of inheritance, and sell shallow Decisions according to the Hidáyah and the Jámi'-ur-rumúz.

There never was a set of young men who stand more in need of good guidance than these poor students of the Muhammadan College. What amount of guidance they get, I have already set forth. Every year under our instruction makes them more confident in their own narrow system of learning, more vicious as to their morals, less fit for any active career in life, and more disloyal to our Government. They hate the sight of an Englishman. When the scandal had grown so public as to render imperative a resident English Professor in the College,[1] he had to be smuggled into it by night. During more than ninety years the Chapters on Holy War against the Infidel have been the favourite studies of the place; and up to 1868 or 1869, I forget the exact date, examination questions were regularly given in this Doctrine of Rebellion. A mosque of fanaticism flourishes almost within the shadow of the College,[2] and the students frequent the Rebel places

[1] At present Mr. Blochmann. Unhappily the Resident English Professor has no jurisdiction over the Arabic or Upper Department.

[2] A *Farází* mosque.

of worship throughout all Calcutta. The present Head Master is the son of one of the leading Doctors whom the Mutiny of 1857 brought to the front, and who expiated his crimes by transportation for life to an island in the Indian Ocean. The library of the learned traitor, after being confiscated by Government, is now lodged in the Calcutta College. Within the last few months, the Resident English Professor had to turn out of the grounds a wandering Arab, who came to 'preach religion,' or, in other words, the doctrines which have cost us three Frontier Wars, and spread a network of conspiracy over the Empire.

After a seven years' training of this sort, we dismiss the Muhammadan youth to the fanatical Eastern Districts whence they came. But unhappily an even sadder tale remains to be told. I do not speak of the last two years during which the Special Commission has been sitting. But there is evidence on record to show that, within a quite recent period, the students brought their courtesans into the College.[1] About twenty-six of them have rooms; and the quarters thus granted by the Government were converted into dens of profligacy. Not content with harbouring what Carlyle calls the unmentionable women, they sunk into those more horrible crimes against nature which Christianity has extirpated from Europe, but which lurk in every great city of India. Within the last five or six years three cases were discovered; how many occurred can never be known.

Even the few among them who, if left to themselves, would try to do well, had no means for obtaining any

[1] It is only just to add that the non-resident English Principal, Colonel Lees, was in no way responsible for these occurrences, and when the courtesan discoveries were made, took steps for rendering their repetition impossible.

sound or practically useful knowledge. In the first place, the time daily devoted to teaching was too short. The fixed hours are from ten to two, from which about twenty minutes must be subtracted in order to allow masters and students to smoke a hooka, known in the College slang as Moses' Rod; and about half an hour for calling the roll,—a ceremony which had to be performed twice a day, as many of the students finally disappeared at twelve o'clock. Some of the more diligent supplement the meagre College curriculum by reading 'religion' in private Musalmán schools outside. Such external studies consist chiefly of the Muhammadan Traditions (*Hadís*), and law-books of the fanatical mediæval stamp,—a sort of learning which fills the youthful brain with windy self-importance, and gives rise to bitter schisms on the most trivial points within the College walls. Not long ago, as the English Resident Professor was going his evening rounds, he heard a tumult in the students' rooms. 'Your religion is all wrong,'[1] and similar phrases, resounded through the corridors, and fierce were the denunciations on all sides. He hurried to the scene of the uproar, and found that one of the students had discovered in a law-book that during prayer the heels should be joined, else the petition has no effect in heaven or on earth. Those who had said their prayers with unclosed heels denounced the discoverer of the new mode as a pernicious heretic; while he and a little band of followers consigned all who prayed in the old fashion to the eternal torments of hell.

Three hours' instruction is as much as they could possibly obtain from the College teachers in the day;—one who has practical acquaintance with it, tells me that the actual time of teaching seldom exceeded two and a

[1] 'Tumhárá ímán t'hík ne.'

half hours. Anything like preparation at home is unknown, and indeed is opposed to Muhammadan ideas. Each master reads out an Arabic sentence, and explains the meanings of the first, second, and third word, and so on till he comes to the end of it. The diligent student writes these meanings between the lines of his text-book, and by easy degrees learns the whole sentence and the interpretation thereof by heart. To teach him how to use the dictionary at home, or to reason out the meaning of a passage on his own account, is an altogether foreign invention, possibly dangerous to his religious faith, and at any rate unknown in the Calcutta College. At the end of seven years the students know certain books by heart, text and interpretation; but if they get a simple manuscript beyond their narrow curriculum, they are in a moment beyond their depth. Such a teaching, it may well be supposed, produces an intolerant contempt for anything which they have not learned. The very nothingness of their acquirements makes them more conceited. They know as an absolute truth that the Arabic grammar, law, rhetoric, and logic, comprise all that is worth knowing upon earth. They have learned that the most extensive kingdoms in the world are, first Arabia, then England, France, and Russia, and that the largest town, next to Mecca, Medina, and Cairo, is London. *Au reste*, the English are Infidels, and will find themselves in a very hot place in the next world. To this vast accumulation of wisdom what more could be added? When a late Principal tried to introduce profane science, even through the medium of their own Urdu, were they not amply justified in pelting him with brick-bats and rotten mangoes?

I have dwelt on these painful details, because I believe

it most important, now that the Government has awakened to the necessity of really educating the Musalmáns, that it should avoid a system which has brought failure upon its one great previous attempt. The Calcutta Muhammadan College has been practically left in the hands of the Muhammadans themselves, and it is under their management that it has proved such a scandal and disgrace. At first our tenderness, and afterwards our indifference, to the waning fortunes of the Musalmán community, prevented the Government from interfering with an institution which it knew to be inefficient, but which it did not see very clearly how to amend. A hundred years of native management has moulded the system to suit the prejudices rather than the wants of the Muhammadans. Our one great fault has been, that we have left the Muhammadan College too much to the Muhammadans themselves. As early as 1819 this was clearly perceived, but the Government of that day went on hoping against hope that a merely nominal control by a European Secretary would in time suffice. The same unwillingness to interfere has characterized and has baffled all the efforts at reform during the past twenty years. When a Principal was at length appointed, his office was an honorary and a nominal one; when a Resident Professor was finally introduced, his jurisdiction stopped short at the Department in which it was most needed.

A recent State Paper complained that only in Northern India do the Muhammadans contribute a fair share, either in numbers or money, to our Schools. The answer lies on the surface. In Bengal, both the more pious and the wealthier families, such as the Nákhudás of Calcutta, will have nothing to do with institutions which do not teach Persian or Arabic, and in which the religious faith of their children might be sapped by infidel Hindu masters. The middle-class does send its boys to our schools; but in Bengal the middle-class of Musalmáns is so thin as to have but slight effect one way or the other. The lower-class Muhammadans have never been reached by our system of Public Instruction, although I have known Missionary Schools such as those of the Rev. James Long full of them. The fanatical, seething masses of the Musalmán peasantry in Eastern Bengal remain beyond the pale of English education or English influence.

Yet I believe that an efficient system of education for all classes of the Musalmán community might be organised at a very small charge to the State. Such a system would have to provide for low-class, middle-class, and high-class instruction. With regard to the first, a liberal construction of the existing Grant-in-Aid Rules would almost suffice. It is not more money that is needed, so much as a consideration of the special wants of the Musalmáns. Government has wisely declared that it will not assist two schools within five miles of each other, for such assistance would produce an unprofitable rivalry at the cost of the State. The astute Hindu, in this as in all other matters, has been first in the field. He has covered the country with schools admirably adapted to the wants of his own community, but wholly unsuited to the requirements of the Muhammadans. The five miles rule, therefore, should be relaxed so as to allow a State grant to Musalmán schools within that distance of existing Hindu ones. Where separate institutions are not needed, Government might make provision for the Musalmáns, by appointing a Muhammadan teacher to the existing Hindu school. Such

Musalmán teachers could be had at five shillings a week.

With regard to the fanatical Eastern Districts, however, I think it would well repay Government to create a special machinery for reaching the Musalmán peasantry. Such machinery was at one time found requisite for the Hindus. Lord Hardinge instituted a number of schools in order to extend education into Districts where there was no self-supporting demand for it. Of these schools thirty-eight survived in the Educational Division of Bengal, that I had in my charge in 1866. They cost the Government over £1100 a year, besides the fees, which amounted only to £267, and were in no sense self-supporting. But it is difficult to overrate the good that these schools have done. Wherever the peasantry were too ignorant, too poor, or too bigoted to set agoing a school under the Grant-in-Aid Rules, one of the Hardinge Institutions was temporarily established. At first the villagers got their education for almost nothing; but by degrees, as the presence of an educated class created a demand for further education, the fees were raised. In a few years the self-supporting element was thus introduced, a higher class of school was formed, and the cheap Hardinge School was transferred to some more backward part of the country. In this way education has been thrown out deeper and deeper into the jungles of South-Western Bengal.[1]

I think the same might now be done for the fanatical Eastern Districts. The Grant-in-Aid Rules will not reach a population hereditarily disaffected to our Government, and averse to our system of instruction. But fifty cheap

[1] In 1865–66 there were 283 schools, with an attendance of 16,043 pupils, in the South-Western Division.

schools, with low-paid Musalmán teachers, to which Government contributed the larger part of the expense, would in a single generation change the popular tone of Eastern Bengal. Such Institutions would have but a small success at first. But they would gradually attract not merely the Musalmán peasant youth,[1] but also the Musalmán teachers, who now earn a precarious livelihood on their own account; and to whom an additional five shillings a week from Government would be an independent fortune. We should thus enlist on our side the very class which is at present most persistently bitter against us.

So much for the lower-class education of the Musalmáns. With regard to their middle-class instruction a still smaller change would be required. The officer in charge of the Wahábi prosecutions has already urged that Muhammadan teachers (*Maulavís*) should be appointed to each of the District Government Schools, and this would suffice. Such teachers should instruct in the usual branches of education through the Urdu vernacular, and give a thorough knowledge of that language, besides an acquaintance with Persian, and perhaps a little Arabic. The prevailing tone of a District Government School might be safely left to itself to produce a desire of learning English among the Musalmán boys who frequented it.

These charges would cost little, but a complete and an efficient system of higher-class Muhammadan education would cost the State not one penny. The sum set apart by Warren Hastings for the Calcutta Musalmán College, and the ample endowments of the Hugli Institu-

[1] The attendance on the 38 'Hardinge and Model Schools' in the South-Western Division rose from 1431 in 1861–62, to 2034 in 1865–66, the year of my Report. The cost per pupil during the same period decreased from 12s. 6d. to 8s. 6d.

tion, would, if properly applied, amply suffice. The funds which we at present misappropriate to maintain an English College should henceforth be honestly devoted to the purpose for which the testator left them. Whether one really good College would not be better than two, and whether it should be fixed in Calcutta, or at Hugli, which is only twenty-four miles off by railway, are matters of detail on which I need not enter here. The actual instruction might for the most part be conducted by Muhammadan teachers as at present; but each College should have a Resident European Principal acquainted with Arabic, and capable both of supervising his subordinates and of enforcing their respect. The emoluments of the position, say from £1200 to £1500 a year, would command an adequate order of scholarship from the English or German Universities.

Such higher-class education would consist not of two distinct branches, as in the Calcutta College, in the Upper of which the student forgets whatever he has learned in the Lower, but of a well-planned unbroken curriculum. The present Upper or Arabic Department could be turned into an Anglo-Arabic one, and form a well-amalgamated extension of the Lower or Anglo-Persian branch. A Musalmán boy would thus pass by easy transitions from the District Government School, through the two College Departments, to the highest branches of learning. It is more than doubtful whether the Muhammadan Law should be taught as a regular study, incumbent on all. It certainly should not be made the chief object of instruction. For the Muhammadan Law means the Muhammadan religion—that religion, too, at a time when its followers looked upon the whole earth as their lawful prey, and before they had learned the duties of modern Musalmán States in alliance with, or in subjection to, a Christian Government. It would not be wise to do away altogether with the teachers of the Law, for its total abolition would imperil the popularity of the College with the present generation of Musalmáns. Yet it should be remembered that our original reason for encouraging Muhammadan Law, to wit, the production of qualified Musalmán Law Officers, has ceased to exist. The study no longer answers any requirement of the Government, nor does it offer to its students any career in life. An adequate knowledge of it could be given in separate lectures, somewhat as the Hindu Law is taught at the Calcutta University. For the present daily drill in the Code of Islám, might be substituted Arabic or Persian literature, and the study of Western science through the medium of Urdu.

In this way we should develope a rising generation of Muhammadans, no longer learned in their own narrow learning, nor imbued solely with the bitter doctrines of their mediæval Law, but tinctured with the sober and genial knowledge of the West. At the same time they would have a sufficient acquaintance with their religious code to command the respect of their own community, while an English training would secure them an entry into the lucrative walks of life.

For the lower and middle class education of the Musalmáns, a special Deputy Inspector of Schools belonging to their own faith would be required. Such an officer might be obtained for £200 a year. One of his first duties should be to find out and report on the Musalmán schools and colleges[1] under native management. An excellent private institution of this sort, with an attendance of 110

[1] Madrasehs.

boys, exists in Calcutta, but can get no Grant-in-Aid. Another, founded by Warren Hastings, survives not far off in a village to the west of Hourah, but does nothing. A third lingers near Maimári, on the East India Railway; a fourth at Sasseram. Similar establishments drag on an obscure existence wholly unknown to our Educational Inspectors. In some of them, I believe, a fair degree of efficiency is maintained, and it would be well to find out if anything is to be learned from the system they pursue. I do not think that they would submit to regular supervision by English officers, but many of them would agree to the visits of a Deputy Inspector of their own faith, as the easy condition of a Grant-in-Aid. We should thus enlist the most seditious Institutions in Bengal on the side, if not of loyalty, at least of peace and order. For the present puerile follies which the Musalmáns read in their schools, a series of well-chosen and well-edited Text-books should be issued. The Colleges might be safely left to the care of their English Principals; and for these ample funds exist, if properly applied, without costing an extra shilling to the State.

We should thus at length have the Muhammadan youth educated upon our own plan. Without interfering in any way with their religion, and in the very process of enabling them to learn their religious duties, we should render that religion perhaps less sincere, but certainly less fanatical. The rising generation of Muhammadans would tread the steps which have conducted the Hindus, not long ago the most bigoted nation on earth, into their present state of easy tolerance. Such a tolerance implies a less earnest belief than their fathers had; but it has freed them, as it would liberate the Musalmáns, from the cruelties which they inflicted, the crimes which they perpetrated, and the miseries which they endured, in the name of a mistaken religion. I do not permit myself here to touch upon the means by which, through a state of indifference, the Hindus and Musalmáns alike may yet reach a higher level of belief. But I firmly believe that that day will come, and that our system of education, which has hitherto produced only negative virtues, is the first stage towards it. Hitherto the English in India have been but poor Iconoclasts after all.

Meanwhile it remains for Government, while sternly putting down disaffection among the Bengal Muhammadans, to deprive them of every excuse for it. It has to make amends to them, not only for the decay in which our conquest and changed administration have involved their community, but also for the want of sympathy which has rendered their ruin less bearable and more complete. Its dealings with the disloyal section of the Musalmáns should be managed so as not only to commend themselves to public justice, but also to public opinion. The unskilful conduct of a well-merited condemnation[1] left for centuries a stain on the memory of the most virtuous Emperor of Rome. Hitherto we have shed no blood, except on the field of battle, and the result has been a crop of Wahábi apostates instead of an army of Wahábi martyrs. At the moment I write this page, the infamous Meat-Supplier of the British Troops,[2] who was condemned to death in 1864, is giving evidence at Patna against the brethren of his former faith. Had his original sentence been carried out, thousands of devotees would every year be making a pilgrimage to his tomb. A death

[1] That of the Viceroy of Africa, the Notary Gaudentius, and the tyrant Duke of Egypt, under Julian.

[2] Muhammad Sháfí'.

in the cause of religion has in all ages sufficed to illuminate a life of infamy. The fortunes of an even viler Meat-Supplier to the Army than our Dehli butcher, stand out in history to warn the Government against capital sentences, which its Musalmán subjects would regard as religious executions. It should never forget how George of Cappadocia, after a life of obloquy as a parasite, as a defaulting bacon-contractor to the Roman Troops, and as a dissolute prelate, obtained an apotheosis by an unwilling death, and became Saint George of Merry England.

# APPENDICES.

## APPENDIX I.

### DECISION OF THE MECCA LAW DOCTORS

*(the Heads of the three Great Musalmán Sects).*

QUESTION.

'What is your opinion (may your greatness continue for ever) on this question; whether the country of Hindustán, the rulers of which are Christians, and who do not interfere with all the injunctions of Islám, such as the ordinary daily Prayers, the Prayers of the two 'Ids, etc., but do authorize departure from a few of the injunctions of Islám, such as the permission to inherit the property of the Muhammadan ancestor to one who changes his religion (being that of his ancestors), and becomes a Christian, is Dár-ul-Islám or not? Answer the above, for which God will reward you.'

ANSWER No. I.

'All praises are due to the Almighty, who is the Lord of all the Creation!

O Almighty, increase my knowledge!

*As long as even some of the peculiar observances of Islám prevail in it, it is the Dár-ul-Islám.*

The Almighty is Omniscient, Pure and High!

This is the *Order* passed by one who hopes for the secret favour of the Almighty, who praises God, and prays for blessings and peace on his Prophet.

(Signed) JAMAL IBN ABDULLAH SHEIKH OMAR UL-HANAFI, the present Mufti of Mecca (the Honoured). May God favour him and his father.'

ANSWER No. II.

'All praises are due to God, who is One; and may the blessings of God be showered upon our Chief, Muhammad, and upon his descendants and companions, and upon the followers of his Faith!

O God! I require guidance from Thee in righteousness.

*Yes! As long as even some of the peculiar observances of Islám prevail in it, it is Dár-ul-Islám.*

The Almighty is Omniscient, Pure and High!

This is written by one who hopes for salvation from the God of mercy. May God forgive him, and his parents and preceptors, and brothers and friends, and all Muhammadans.

(Signed) AHMAD IBN ZAINI DAHLAN, Mufti of the Sháfi'í Sect of Mecca (the Protected).

ANSWER No. III.

'All praises are due to God, who is One! O! Almighty! increase my knowledge!

*It is written in the Commentary of Dasoki that a Country of Islám does not become Dár-ul-Harb as soon as it passes into the hands of the Infidels, but only when all or most of the injunctions of Islám disappear therefrom.*

God is Omniscient! May the blessings of God be showered upon our Chief, Muhammad, and on his descendants and companions.

(Signed) Written by HUSAIN IBN IBRAHIM, Mufti of the Málikí Sect of Mecca (the Illustrious).'

---

## APPENDIX II.

### THE DECISION OF THE LAW DOCTORS OF NORTHERN INDIA.

TRANSLATION OF THE ISTIFTA OR QUESTION, PUT BY SAYYID AMIR HUSAIN, PERSONAL ASSISTANT TO THE COMMISSIONER OF BHAGALPUR.

What is your Decision, O men of learning and expounders of the law of Islám, in the following?—

Whether a Jihád is lawful in India, a country formerly held by a Muhammadan ruler, and now held under the sway of a Christian Government, where the said Christian Ruler does in no way interfere with his Muhammadan subjects in the Rites prescribed by their Religion, such as Praying, Fasting, Pilgrimage, Zakát, Friday Prayer, and Jama'at, and gives them fullest protection and liberty in the above respects in the same way as a Muhammadan Ruler would do, and where the Muhammadan subjects have no strength and means to fight with their rulers; on the contrary, there is every chance of the war, if waged, ending with a defeat, and thereby causing an indignity to Islám.

Please answer, quoting your authority.

Fatwa dated the 17th Rabí'-us-sání, or Rabí' II., 1287 H., corresponding with the 17th July 1870.

The Musalmáns here are protected by Christians, and there is no Jihád in a country where protection is afforded, as the absence of protection and liberty between Musalmáns and Infidels is essential in a religious war, and that condition does not exist here. Besides, it is necessary that there should be a probability of victory to Musalmán and glory to the Indians. If there be no such probability, the Jihád is unlawful.

Here the Maulavís quote Arabic passages from Manháj-ul-Ghaffár and the Fatáwi-i-Alamgírí, supporting the above decision.

Seals of
MAULAVI ALI MUHAMMAD, of Lucknow;
MAULAVI ABD-UL-HAI, of Lucknow;
MAULAVI FAZLULLAH, of Lucknow;
MUHAMMAD NAIM, of Lucknow;
MAULAVI RAHMATULLAH, of Lucknow;
MAULAVI KUTAB-UD-DIN, of Dehli;
MAULAVI LUTFULLAH, of Rampur;
*and others.*

---

## APPENDIX III.

### DECISION OF THE CALCUTTA MUHAMMADAN SOCIETY.

After declaring, in opposition to the northern Law Doctors, that India *is* a Dár-ul-Islám, Maulaví Karamat Alí proceeded thus:

'The second question is, "Whether it is lawful in this Country to make *Jihád* or not." This has been solved together with the first. For *Jihád* can by no means be lawfully made in Dár-ul-Islám. This is so evident that it requires no argument or authority to support it. Now, if any misguided wretch, owing to his perverse fortune, were to wage war against the Ruling Powers of this Country, British India; such war would be rightly pronounced rebellion; and rebellion is strictly forbidden by the Muhammadan Law. Therefore such war will likewise be unlawful; and in case any one would wage such war, the Muhammadan subjects would be bound to assist their Rulers, and, in conjunction with their Rulers, to fight with such rebels. The above has been clearly laid down in the Fatáwi-i-Alamgírí.'